COBBLED STREETS
&
PENNY SWEETS

COBBLED STREETS
&
PENNY SWEETS

Happy Times and Hardship in
Post-War Britain

YVONNE YOUNG

JOHN BLAKE

Published by John Blake Publishing,
2.25, The Plaza,
535 Kings Road,
Chelsea Harbour,
London SW10 0SZ

www.johnblakebooks.com

www.facebook.com/johnblakebooks 🔘
twitter.com/jblakebooks 🔘

This edition first published in 2019

ISBN: 978 1 78946 012 4

British Library Cataloguing-in-Publication Data:

A catalogue record for this book is available from the British Library.

Typeset by www.envydesign.co.uk

Printed and bound in Great Britain by Clays Ltd, Elcograf S.p.A.

1 3 5 7 9 10 8 6 4 2

John Blake Publishing is an imprint of Bonnier Books UK
www.bonnierbooks.co.uk

For Jimmy Forsyth, Newcastle's adopted
Geordie photographer

Contents

CHAPTER ONE

The Sun Has Got
His Hat On

When your parents collect things from the past in an old cardboard box, they have no idea that, in time, you will piece their story together. The receipt for Mam's wedding ring, purchased at The Northern Goldsmiths, 85 & 87 Westgate Road, Newcastle upon Tyne, price £3.00, 'The Ring Shop For The World' dated 29 September 1951 (I was born on 24 February 1952).

When I was around five years old I looked at a photo of my parents in their wedding gear.

'Where was I?'

'You weren't here yet.'

Whatever did they mean, how could they be somewhere without me? This was disgraceful. If I wasn't there yet, well, where was I? Questions they couldn't answer, but I was there alright. I never understood why being a single mother was frowned upon, but a couple, like my parents, who had married while the bride was pregnant was acceptable. Both these women were 'up the stick', the local term, yet the veneer of respectability was what mattered to the community.

Mam and Dad moved in with Nana, Dad's mother, at 17 Maria Street, one of the dozens of back-to-backs which steeply sloped down towards Scotswood Road. Five doors up from Vickers Armstrong's garage and just behind their armament factories. The men in the garage were forever running out to chase kids for throwing stones onto the corrugated steel roof. During World War II, when women were employed to take on the work of men called away, everything was covered in dust and folks had to hold down the china when a tank was on the loose, up one of the streets on a test run. The bombs were filled with explosives, which the women were responsible for putting inside, and this turned their hair and skin yellow. They were nicknamed 'Canary Girls'. It was a very dangerous job as they fixed the caps down on the bombs and there was always a chance the bombs could go off. The yellow from handling these explosives wore off eventually but there were tales of pregnant women who gave birth to yellow babies. The effects of colouration of the babies' skin wore off after a couple of weeks, but I believe that the workers suffered skin complaints and breathing difficulties because of the work.

After the men returned from active service, most of these women lost their jobs, but there wasn't a great deal of re-organisation as few men were conscripted since the work at

Vickers was regarded as being vital to the war effort. It had been a boom time for the company and the shipyards were replacing bombed vessels. There was plenty of work and wages were good, but when nationalisation of shipbuilding and aircraft took place in 1967 over 50 per cent of the company was lost and they were told not to depend on armaments, so work was moved away from Elswick and different ways of working introduced. (They did manufacture tractors for a while, and even one prototype for a doll's pram, but none of their new products reached the phenomenal heights of production during wartime and into the 1950s.)

Nana's place was a downstairs flat opposite a bomb site – apparently, the German airmen were aiming for the factories. Vickers had made our area a prime target for the Luftwaffe. In our area alone, almost 400 people were killed by bombs from German planes between 1940 and 1941, as they tried to destroy our tanks, armaments and shipping but hit local homes instead. Even during my childhood in the 1950s, there was still a lot of damage to buildings around the West End of Newcastle. We played among the rubble, looking for bits of old china. Sometimes we came across a blue piece but even more prized was anything with gold on it.

Scotswood Road was famous for its forty-six pubs, most of them built on the corner of another street. It was said that rates were more expensive on the main road so by being built on the corner, publicans could lay claim to their address off-road. So pubs mingled in with the corner shops and fish-and-chip shops.

Music was a feature in our flat as my parents both enjoyed musicals. Dad favoured *My Fair Lady* and *Gigi*, while Mam sang songs from *South Pacific* and *Can-Can*. I still remember, young as I was, feeling acute embarrassment as I became aware that they were watching me as I flounced around while singing one of those songs. I hid behind a chair and they laughed all the more. But while Mam might have laughed at my attempts to warble, she herself wasn't so keen to perform when anyone else was watching.

The only party I had at home was around the same year: some children from our street were invited with their mothers and we ate egg-and-tomato sandwiches. We had a huge brown earthenware teapot which had a handle above the spout – when full, it would have been impossible to hold upright with the regular handle alone. Mam had never actually used it before and put far too much tea in (someone observed that it was like Spanish tea). A game of Ring o' Roses was suggested and the mothers joined hands with us kids, but none of them wanted to sing, so it all descended into frustration.

'Oh, just play among yourselves. Here, eat some bullets!'

A friend of mine, Mary, came to live in the area from Scotland when she was seven years of age. After being at the school for just one week, she came home crying.

'Mammy, there's a girl in my class has got a gun.'

'Have you seen it?' her mother asked.

'No, but she keeps asking me if I have any bullets.'

'Bullets' was a north-eastern term for sweets in general. The Black Bullet, a popular minty-tasting confection shaped like

4

little balls, probably started this adaptation. There were many children who were bitterly disappointed while waiting for a parent to return from a first day making bullets at Vickers armament factory, only to be informed they were made of metal, not candy.

Derelict houses were a magnet for us kids, no safety fencing or blocked-off entrances. We dared each other to go upstairs and walk around the skirting boards of rooms with massive holes in the middle of the floor and blown bricks staring up at us. An old church on the corner of a street was under compulsory purchase. Huge oak doors hung off their hinges and when we ventured inside, most of the flooring on the far side was caved in. On further inspection, we saw there was a flood of water underneath – someone must have been in for the copper piping.

I have no memory of Nana, but Mam said that she had infinite patience with me, putting my bootees on when I kept pulling them off. Every Sunday, she attended St Aidan's Church and enjoyed voluntary work. My grandfather Charles died in 1940. He had moved to Newcastle in 1904 from Falmouth, where he had been a mariner, so he slotted right into working on ships at Vickers-Armstrong engineering works.

Many of the pubs on the Scotswood Road were named after machinery or armament from the factories: The Gun, The Hydraulic Crane, The Rifle, The Forge Hammer and The Mechanics, etc. I loved listening to my Uncle Tom's stories. He remembered that Grandad rigged a bracket on the wall in the backyard to make nets and tents to sell for extra money. More than likely, the materials were gathered from the workplace.

All of the homes in the area were painted grey, dark green or brown – battleship colours.

I enjoyed listening to tales of local characters. There was the rat catcher who called in at the pubs, went into the cellars and placed a lantern with a kipper over the top. He hid in the corner until the rat came sniffing, then grabbed it with his bare hands and chucked it in a hessian sack. The charge to the publican was 4d (2p) for a little rat and 6d (3p) for a large one. If the payment wasn't given, the catcher tipped them all out onto the bar counter – 'Here then, have your rats back!' Sure enough, this would clear the place.

A neighbour had worked in many jobs but took a job in pest control for a while. Folks went past and said, 'There goes the rat catcher.' Everyone knew him because many people had need of his services – in shops, homes and pubs. There were rats in the Co-op, anywhere where there was food. Hundreds of rats ran along the Quayside. A team of eight men laid traps and left them to do their work. Nobody bothered them, people pointed, 'They're in there' and then went away. They all said they could never do that job, especially in the cattle market near the river. There was so much blood running among the cobbles, the rats swarmed everywhere. I was shocked when my neighbour told me that sometimes the rats ran up his trouser legs. He had seen bulls being led by herdsmen using sticks to chase them along and joked, 'At least the bulls didn't run up my trouser leg!'

On my way out from the backyard one day I looked along St John's Road, near the cemetery, and was horrified to see a huge black bull belting along the middle of the road. The poor thing had escaped from the abattoir and was covered in foaming sweat, steam pulsing from its nostrils. It was terrified and so was I, so I kept looking but only with my head showing from behind the door. The cattle market employees were hot on the beast's trail in a large wagon. Inside the graveyard they cornered and calmed it down, enticing it into the vehicle with around five heifers. I can't imagine the terror when the unfortunate creature realised that it was headed back from whence it had escaped. These days, animals are stunned in a more humane way compared to the practice adopted back then.

There were many stories of escaped animals. On one occasion a pregnant woman was standing at her front door when a bull ran around the corner of her street, where folks were gathered, chatting. They took one look at the bull and stampeded over the woman to get into her house.

The chimney sweep was a favourite of mine. A father-and-son team visited homes in the area. To me it was fascinating how they carried a long fabric bag, unravelled it and inside were all these poles and a huge circular brush. The bag doubled as a cover to protect flooring from dust and half-covered the fireplace. The sweep slotted all the poles together and the fabulous brush was the crown. I was very curious: what was he doing? What were the poles for? What was going to happen? After every question, he just said, 'Shush!'

Later, I asked, 'Mam, is the sweep called Shush?'

This snake of a man went up the chimney and then the excitement began. I ran outside and half the street was gathered around our back door in the lane. Everyone knew which house the sweep was working in, so word got around. Then the long-awaited event happened: the brush burst forth from the chimney pot, doing its pirouette. A massive cheer would go up. Folks were easily pleased in those days!

Guy Fawkes was another important happening in our lane. Weeks before, us kids would be collecting firewood, old furniture, windfall from trees in the park. The stash was protected at all times, as groups from other lanes would be on the lookout to steal from someone else's supply. We saved up to buy a box of fireworks and quite shockingly, compared to safety standards today, children were allowed to buy loose bangers and Catherine wheels from local shops. On the day, wood was stacked in a kind of wigwam shape and any Guys which had been made from old clothes and stuffed with newspaper were placed on top. The Guys were used beforehand to collect money for fireworks. Kids stood outside the pubs, hoping to catch any passing drunk who might put his hand in his pocket.

'Penny for the Guy, Mister, please.'

Secretly, we hoped by chance they might be so intoxicated that as they scratted through their change, a two-bob bit might be mistaken for a penny.

Lanes were quite narrow as housing wasn't built to accommodate cars in those days and one drawback of the bonfire being too close to back doors resulted in the blistering and popping of paint. But it didn't matter, people simply redecorated. Guy Fawkes Night was seen as something that just happened, it was tradition and nobody ever mentioned that it should be banned. Catherine wheels were nailed to doors, rockets were stood inside milk bottles and 'set off', younger children held sparklers. It was a community gathering and people put potatoes and chestnuts in the fire to bake. Mind you, they didn't taste all that good! They were left to cool down and ended up tasting charred and rubbery, nothing like the Nat King Cole song had led me to believe!

There were church processions on Sundays, which started off at Condercum Road (Condercum is a Roman word as they built a fort at the top of the road, it means 'place with a good view'). From there you can see right across the valley and rolling over the River Tyne towards Gateshead. Services were held in the street and at Easter, a pastor would offer his sermon from the back of a flatbed lorry. Women wore hats complete with hatpin or a head square as an alternative. Mam never attended these gatherings as there wasn't a religious bone in her body, although she did possess a wide range of headscarves. Some had very elaborate patterns and among her collection were lighthouses, enormous flowers and sailing ships.

Women enjoyed playing darts in the pub and had their own teams. Folks would sing around the piano and continue singing up the street after closing time. After a while chatting outside someone's home, a suggestion was made to continue inside. The rug was rolled back and they danced and sang until the early hours. Remember, this was a time when folks didn't rely on TV or digital devices for entertainment and storytelling was a staple of the community. I liked nothing better than listening to the adults having a chinwag about the good old days, sharing family stories and gossiping.

Children played out until they were forced to go inside for the night, crafts and knitting were encouraged and the lads would help with taking care of the pigeons in the cree [a hut or pen] or learn how to make tools or household items. There were joiners, fitters, electricians, plumbers and other tradesmen on every street. Many a home, including mine, used items such as the guard for the fireplace (or a 'bleezer' as we called it), poker and toasting fork courtesy of the local metal works.

The local general dealer shops on Adelaide Terrace smelled of paraffin, mothballs and bundles of sticks. When you entered you were greeted by beautiful oak counters and assistants behind them who knew their stuff. The walls of the haberdashery store were lined with wooden doors with glass panels and tiny little drawers which held ribbons, buttons and metal zips. Women who wanted to knit a jumper asked at the wool shop if they could buy a ball a week – 'Put the balls away'. This meant they had worked out how many balls were needed, then collected one a week, paying as they knitted. Folks couldn't afford to buy everything at once. Tobacconists sold single cigarettes to those who couldn't afford the pack and of course, most shops offered 'on tick' to run up a tab.

If someone was wearing a rather tatty garment, another might comment, 'Where did you get that, Paddy's Market?' This referred to a practice on the Quayside where second-hand clothes (now known as 'pre-loved'!) could be bought for a few pennies. Often they were strewn on the pavement for folks to forage through – there might be a coat better than the one they were wearing. There were second-hand shops in the area for clothing, bric-a-brac and furniture.

On Sundays the larger expanse of the Quayside was lined with stalls. I recall that rabbits, kittens and budgies were sold, along with low-priced foods and clothing, toys, etc. Sometimes an escapologist would entertain the crowds – tales abounded of a time when he couldn't get out of the sack, which was wrapped in chains. Apparently, he kept the key to a large padlock between his teeth and he had dropped it!

An old pitman used to walk over the Chain Bridge to a pub on the other side of the River Tyne, but occasionally got into a punch-up with other drinkers. One morning, his jacket was found down by the river and no sign of him. A search was made but he wasn't found, so a couple of weeks later, a memorial service was held – people assumed he had drowned. However, he had got into a fight with some Dutch bargemen, who were taking coal away from Newcastle, so as he was drunk, they threw him onto the boat. He had to wait until they made a return visit to this city to get home. It didn't half cause a fuss!

In those days it was necessary for every house-proud housewife to 'donkey stone the front step'. In other words, they scrubbed it clean on their hands and knees, bucket at the side, before a yellow rubbing stone was applied. You weren't allowed to step on it when it was newly done. The fanlight received the same diligent attention – apparently, a dirty step and fanlight meant you had a dirty home. Folks really took a pride in their meagre dwelling places. The women were regularly seen out on the street, wearing Paisley pinnies with scarves tied with a knot at the front, covering their hair curlers (working-class turban style), sweeping their part of the path. Of course, this was also an excuse to gossip (known as 'gassing'). They would stand around gassing about this one or that one:

'Who does she think she is, the cat's mother?'

'Aye, man, aal fur coat and nee knickers!'

Or:

'What's she doing, walking up the road with him?'

'Wonder if there's anything going on?'

Mam used to say, 'Look at those two, pulling someone to bits, no doubt!' But it was perfectly OK when she was doing it herself.

I became increasingly interested in local sayings and their origins as I tuned in to their conversations:

'These things are sent to try us' – A particular favourite of Mam's, which seemed to have a religious connotation.

'He looks like the Wild Man of Borneo' – I have no idea of the origins of this one, only that it had a similar meaning to Paddy's Market.

Also:

'He looks like he's been dragged through a hedge backwards'

None of them flattering, but a phrase which defies logic, usually said to children after some naughtiness, was: 'You'll be laughing on the other side of your face when I get my hands on you!'

None of our neighbours had carpets, you were lucky if you had a rug in the centre of the floor. Lino or 'oil cloth' (some called it 'Tarry toot') with black bitumen in it was popular and cheap, although it cracked easily. Any old bits were used on the bonfire on 5 November – very dangerous stuff as it dripped red-hot and if any got on your skin, it left a scar. The dining table was usually set square in the middle of the room. Flypapers were fixed to the light fitting, if you had one, as bare bulbs were commonplace in Benwell due to the expense of buying lampshades. It was appalling to sit there eating food while numerous flies wriggled their last on the brown sticky surface. Curtains were strung up on a wire and a half-net from the middle of the sash window prevented nosy neighbours from 'knowing your business'.

The kitchen led into the backyard, where the tin bath lodged on a nail. When it rained, it was impossible to get a good night's sleep for the continual plinking sounds. The outside toilet – 'the netty' – was next to the coal house: a hatch from the lane ensured that the coal man could deposit the family's supply straight in there. The coal men hauled huge hessian sacks of the stuff over one shoulder from the lorry. A family down on their luck could buy a bucketful to keep them going, otherwise they would chop up the furniture during the winter. It was possible to ascertain whose dad worked for the Coal Board as a pyramid of the black gold was deposited outside their door in the lane. While outdoors toilets were usually whitewashed once a year, an extra-fastidious housewife would also whitewash the coal house.

When the coal van arrived, mothers sent their children out: 'Stand there and count the bags in!'

I never understood why everyone did their washing on Mondays and placed it on long lines, criss-crossed over the lane. This was the day the coal van called so the women ran out with their props held aloft to allow it through. But woe betide any driver who didn't give a warning and sailed straight through those white sheets. Angry females would beat the side of the lorry with their rolled-up sleeves. The women were also out in force if us kids decided on a game of 'Run Through'. It was a great feeling to charge into the freshly laundered cotton and feel the flap on our faces. I wonder now how any of those women got any work done between attending to us and the coal men.

According to Uncle Tom, Grandad cleared our coal house out and kept his racing pigeons in there. A wagon would call round, up and down the lanes, to pick up pigeons in their baskets to take to the yearly race. The baskets were taken to France where the birds were set free. Once a year, the local Homing Union held a show at the Town Hall, which was very much a social occasion for Grandad and men like him. On one occasion, me and a pal went further west along Edward Gardens to play with our box of chalks. We were well into drawing on the paving stones – a little house, some flowers, a sun with spokes of sunlight emanating from its orb – when an angry-looking man came raging up the walkway towards us.

'You two have done this, haven't you?'

'What, Mister?' I asked.

'You've broken into my aviary and killed all my pigeons! You did it, didn't you? Answer me!'

We were scared, but I said, 'We don't know your pigeons.'

At this he broke down and cried uncontrollably. Through his tears he murmured, 'I know. I'm sorry, it wasn't you, I can see that.'

He turned on his heel and went off sobbing. It was well known that if a man had prize birds and could win the big prize money there might be someone who would want to take out the competition. A fancier called Reggie had an aviary like a little Roman Villa: it was on three sides, with little steps leading up to the fencing on all of them and even tiles on the roof. Most of the fanciers spent the majority of their time there and they also kept allotments on their site to grow vegetables. It was a standing joke if anyone asked when they could speak to a bird man.

'Oh, you'll have to be lucky to catch him at the aviary, he's only there from eight in the morning until eight at night.'

A big queue at the bus stop one Monday morning were treated to an amusing show when a wife was berating her husband in the queue. He was going to work that morning after being at his aviary all weekend, even sleeping there before an important competition.

'Aye, you bugger, and you can stay out again tonight and forever because I'm changing the locks on the door!'

Big money could be made from competitions among the working men. Leek clubs were popular, where men had secret recipes such as feeding Newcastle Brown Ale, as well as other organic matter, to their crops. Rhubarb was grown under a spare tin bath and some men were fortunate enough to have a plot at an allotment a couple of streets away from our house. At dusk, me and my pal Lillian climbed in there to grab a few stalks. It was a lovely experience to poke my nail into the top, drawing the skin the whole way down, a saucer full of sugar lined up to dip into and crunch away.

Mam took on the task of wallpapering but couldn't be bothered to match the patterns or cut off the white border. The sheets weren't metered into the corner, instead, she curved the rolls around the four walls. This came in handy when I was in my cot as I could puncture little holes as far as my height would allow. A curious memory I have of this practice was when I imagined that I saw a little bear dancing in one of the holes. Time after time I returned but it never came back – I think I must have fallen asleep mid-poking.

I remember holding Mam's hand outside of what seemed like a giant double gate with a huge garden behind. A woman on the other side explained that children were not allowed (I was around four). Mam entered and I waited there until she came back. I have since discovered that this place was Little Sisters of the Poor in Elswick. Nuns ran a home for the elderly, supporting folks who could not afford care. Dad never visited her, his own mother. This was left to Mam. Her husband, grandad Charles, had passed away soon after the war, and she had had a hard life working to keep a home for eight children. She died at the age of sixty-eight, but as with so many people from that time, she looks decades older in photos I have seen of her.

After Nana died, they kept the flat on and Mam took work at a factory. Dad was off to work at Adams and Gibbon garage on his pushbike and I was left in the bedroom until Sheila, Mam's friend from up the street, called in to take me to her flat. One morning, I had woken and climbed up to the window, looking out onto the street. It was raining and I was crying, I don't know how long for. Once at Sheila's, much to my shame as I recall this, I lodged myself under her dining table, which had a crossbar linking the legs. Thoroughly enjoying myself, I shouted 'Bugger!' Furious, she tried to catch me as I hopped from one side to the other, shrieking with delight at her rage. She had a stutter, which made it all the more fun. When I was older, I was told that Sheila had answered a call to her front door, leaving her baby daughter in the cot. A fire had broken out and a neighbour came in the back way and took the child to safety. Sheila never got over the shock and this was how she developed her stutter.

We never escape our memories and the guilt accompanying them.

The cardboard box was always a source of delight to me. Dad's wardrobe had a big metal key with 'Tradecraft' embedded in the bow. Access to the box was by way of climbing up the very useful cubbyholes meant for socks and ties, etc. Small photos with thick white borders showed Indian men wearing *dhotis* (a traditional garment) and crouched down over clay pots and ornate archways and Uncle Alfie wearing his cream uniform and pith helmet. *The Guide to Hindustani* was used by my uncle during service but I was quite shocked at the phrases in there, which to me seemed a bit cheeky: 'I have forgotten your name', 'Don't make a noise', 'Get the hot bath ready', 'Bring me shaving water' and even 'This handkerchief is dirty, bring me another'. I couldn't help but think, why didn't they just do it themselves?

There were a couple of medals and a small metal box containing a photo of a soldier, a bullet and a piece of striped ribbon. Dad sitting proudly on a howitzer gun, kissing a bronze statue of a naked woman, and lots of letters. Two were written in German from a woman called Edith. I couldn't understand the language but there were lots of lovely drawings in the borders of horseshoes and bells. If fact, there were quite a few pictures of women – Alice, Fernanda… I wasn't really interested in those.

Mam's wardrobe was where they kept my Easter eggs. Hers didn't have cubbyholes so I used a chair to reach the top shelf. I took the silver paper from the eggs, ate the back and any chocolates inside, then replaced the paper as if everything was in order. Of course, I was only robbing myself.

One Christmas holiday when I was five was a time to remember. Uncle Les came back from Singapore and brought lots of presents. I was given five dolls with rubber bodies and pot heads. By the end of the day, there were five headless bodies! Thumping from one room to another excitedly with a doll under each arm, negotiating the doorframes wasn't my strong point. The adults were preoccupied – it was great to have Les home, but it was marred by the fact that Uncle Alfie had died, only in his twenties after contracting tuberculosis during his service in India, so he never came home.

Among my gifts was a wishing well with a tiny bucket, which went up and down by turning a handle attached to string. Water was poured inside and I had endless fun. A marvellous oven appeared on the dining-room table, with real little tin pans and hollow rings, where some kind of spirit was poured and set alight. I could boil actual water! The drop-down door revealed a metal tray to put things inside. This was something else… only, there was another girl there getting in the way and she wanted to play with *my* oven. No way! I kept shoving her to get in first. Then it was time for this lass and her mother to leave – brilliant! But they were taking the gorgeous appliance with them. What was going on? Mam had a hell of a time explaining it belonged to the girl, whoever she was, and that they had only brought it to show me.

Hmm…

Another toy a pal owned which I always coveted was a Cinderella and Prince wind-up tin toy. When fully wound, the couple, arm in arm, circled around the floor. I never got one of those.

* * *

There was also an old lady nicknamed 'Tickly Annie' who lived a few doors up from us. On leaving her downstairs flat, she would turn the key, then bang and push the door for about five minutes. She would turn at the bottom of the path, go back and push, then pull a few times more. At the bottom of the street, Annie would look puzzled, then go back again to push a few more times. This went on until she finally left the street. On her return, if any bairns were hanging about, she either played a game called 'Got Your Nose', which involved nipping a child's nose and holding her thumb in between her first two digits, or she would 'tickle' them by digging her bony fingers into their ribs. This caused much resentment from the older kids so Annie was usually the first target in a game of 'Knocky Nine Door' – basically knocking on someone's front door, then running away.

Her front room couldn't be viewed from outside because of the huge plants filling the window frame. I was wandering past one day when I noticed a broom handle peering from above the leaves of the central plant. Unbeknown to me, some lads had just knocked on Annie's door and run away. The broom handle sharply disappeared and she was at the open front door, eyes ablaze at me. Not a good sign! I took off down to my place but didn't think to slam the door behind me. Instead, I opted to hide behind, with the door pulled towards me. Tickly Annie whacked her brush repeatedly as I cowered in the corner in fear of my life – she wasn't intent on rib tickling that day. Dad was in, but he thought I was 'only playing'.

My friend Audrey took half a dozen bobbins of thread from

her mother's sewing box to use in a game of Knocky Nine Door. She trailed the thread across the road and fixed each thread to a letterbox, then went back across to hide behind a wall. Once hidden, she pulled and six knockers were sounded. Audrey then rolled her traps up. The women answered and all shared their puzzlement while Audrey chuckled in her hiding place. After staying there for some time, the coast was clear so she headed back home to replace the threads. But one of her victims had brought an item of clothing round to be altered by Audrey's mother. The conversation got around to pesky kids who were disturbing the peace.

'I know what I would do with them!'

When the box was opened and the threads were discovered missing, Audrey's mother shot a glance at her daughter standing there, hands behind her back. Having clicked that she was the culprit, she gave chase.

It wasn't only the women who were handy at making things. Dad often came in from the lane with something he had found. An old inner tube from a tyre would be used to heel our shoes on the cobbler's last, a holding device shaped like a foot that is used to repair shoes. But some items were decidedly odd, such as a single flipper, which he spent a great deal of time cutting the 'flip' off.

'Dad, what are you doing with that?'

'I might find the other one and then I'll have a pair of slippers.'

This was run-of-the-mill stuff in our house but I soon picked up that my friends didn't see it that way. If I asked any of them in, not wanting to commit themselves, they always asked, 'Is your dad in?' before agreeing to enter.

Dad did actually use tyres for their specific purpose when he fixed a puncture on his bike. It would be upended in the sitting room with a bowl of water sat on the lino. He would slide the inner tube through to test for a release of air, then he knew where to fit the glue and patch.

Mam was always off to visit her parents and brothers and sister at Gateshead, or else she was with her pal, Irene. Irene was a huge woman who batted the doors ajar with one hip and had a baby on the other. She had three sons who could never get a word in edgeways for her chatter, her husband was a quiet bloke who was a 'clippy' on the buses. Irene wasn't good with the family finances and like Mam, she couldn't cook for toffee. When the wage packet was handed over on Fridays, she always went to the nearest shop and bought bags of biscuits. People said her kids were 'pasty-looking'. The baby would be propped up in his pram with reins on and given endless biscuits and bits of bread, which congealed on his legs and made a little carpet inside the pram. James, the middle child, stuffed a peanut up each nostril and it was 'a devil to get them out'.

We consumed a fair amount of biscuits too, the favourites being fig rolls, Jaffa Cakes and Garibaldi. Sometimes there would be Nice biscuits and there was always a debate on the correct pronunciation, as in 'This is a nice cake' or 'I'm going to Nice for my holidays'. The selection was never deviated from. It was the same with cheese, either Cheddar or Cheshire. Only Cheshire never got its name, we called it

'Crumbly'. Sterilised Puroh milk was always on the table – we didn't own a fridge so the taste was disgusting, and there were floating slimy lumps in it.

Often, we went on day trips to places like Blackpool with Irene, her husband and the boys. We took the usual egg-and-tomato sandwiches, which were always soggy by the time we arrived. Why did they never learn that this would happen and change the fillings? Still, I suppose it was a change from cheese! We also referred to them as 'sand sandwiches' as once our hands dipped in the yellow stuff, it was quickly transferred to food. Predictably, Dad went off on his own – he didn't have friends, didn't make any or want to either. The only time he engaged us in conversation was to complain about any cold or flu symptoms he had. It was a standing joke between Mam and Irene, they laughed when they saw his sickbed routine and would cry, 'Bring out your dead!' at his performance.

The Beechams Powders would appear, then he boiled bottled fizzy lemonade and added sliced fresh lemons to it. Vick was dolloped into a bowl of hot water. He then hid himself under a towel and when he surfaced, we had to listen to the analysis of who could have passed the cold on to him, where and how. Mam and Irene almost took to their beds trying to suppress their laughter. Dad's head would also be in his *Doctor's Answers* book. He tried Mam's patience one day when he announced, 'I think I've got typhoid.'

'Don't be so bloody stupid, Ken! You wouldn't be sitting there like that if you had.'

'But the symptoms point to...'

'Oh, bugger off, man!'

It was no comedy when I first experienced Dad's reaction to one of his 'breathing attacks'. I was at home when he started clasping at his chest as if he was having a heart attack so I ran along to the family doctor's surgery in Ethel Street. The housekeeper answered and said she would pass the message on. I was screaming that this was an emergency (I was to discover that there would be many 'emergencies' – usually when Dad couldn't get his own way or there was something he couldn't change). He would brood about it until he had a panic attack, or passed out. On this occasion, it was my mother's social life – she was trying to have one, visiting her friends' or relatives' houses. When everything was going Dad's way, we didn't have the dramas, but we still heard the usual stories when he had a cold:

'I could have got it from that woman on the bus who sneezed and didn't cover her mouth.'

Or:

'It was probably that man who was blowing his nose in Marks & Spencer – I could have bought a tin that he touched.'

And I didn't escape: if I suffered a cold, Vick was shoved up my nose too and I was forced under the towel over a dish. I endured countless cups of boiled lemonade and was given liquid paraffin, Milk of Magnesia and cod liver oil, but I can't say it turned me into a hypochondriac, thankfully.

Perhaps inevitably, Mam began biting her nails. She tried a preparation called Bitter Alice, but she was so far gone with stress that she simply became immune to the taste. When she developed a rash on her arms which itched, the doctor prescribed a coconut cream, but that didn't help either – there was no prescription to solve Dad.

He worked for a series of garages. Whenever I think of him, a mop of dark wavy hair being flicked away from his eyes with a shake of the head, bicycle clips and the smell of petrol comes into my head. His nickname was 'Doddy' as he resembled the comedian Ken Dodd (without the protruding teeth). Dad would often walk out of a job, swearing at his employers if he had a disagreement about something that didn't suit him, much to Mam's great distress. A lad who used to be in my class at school – Charlie (his dad worked at the same garage) – once said that Dad got in trouble for threatening the boss with a screwdriver (Dad's substitute for Ken Dodd's tickling stick, perhaps). At this time he was continually being sacked from jobs for one reason or another. He didn't appreciate being told what to do.

I still have the letter which was delivered to the garage where he worked at the time. It read:

> *Southern Counties Garages Ltd,*
> *'Doddy', Panel Shop, Rossleigh Garage Ltd., Fourth Street, Newcastle.*
> *Dear Sir,*
> *I must apologise for this address on this envelope, but we have no other way of contacting you. We were informed by Mr Backshall that you would be interested in a job at a garage in this area. We can offer you*

a job as a fitter in our accident repair shop. Should you prove acceptable, we are prepared to pay the going hourly rate, plus a bonus each week. Most of our staff work about forty-eight hours a week, eight of which are at overtime rate. We could arrange an interview when it would be most suitable to yourself. We would be prepared to refund your travelling expenses after the interview. We await your reply and hope we can come to some mutually agreeable arrangement.

Yours faithfully,

R. Cheeseman

Body-shop Manager

But Dad didn't attend. He said that the extra working hours put him off. Forty was his limit and no amount of persuasion from Mam convinced him otherwise. She thought that even if he worked extra for a few years, it would set them up. But no.

* * *

There was generally a woman in the street who was ready to organise a trip out. The bus would be booked and everyone paid their share. Once on the beach, a plateau of sand was made and a tablecloth placed over the top. Many families took their own teapot to be filled with boiling water from a nearby café. As I've said, the sandwiches were usually egg and tomato. Us kids referred to them as 'soggies' – by the time you got there, the tomato had soaked into the egg and bread – or 'sand sandwiches'.

If I went to plodge at the sea's edge, my legs got wet and when Mam dried me, it was like little razor blades were cutting my legs from sand, which had stuck to the skin. I liked it far better when Dad was there as he picked me from the water and carried me back to be dried humanely. They both enjoyed singing: 'Volare' for Dad and she'd be belting out 'King Creole'.

Mam was well into her sunbathing routine and so Dad would wander off on a walk – he never went to the pub like the other men. I would either wind up in the Lost Children hut or latch onto someone else's mother for the day. He would snap an apple in half by prising his thumbs into the top and we shared half each, then he went for his walk. On one occasion he returned and I was nowhere to be found. The tide was coming in and so he scoured the place. Luckily for me, he checked the caves on Cullercoats beach behind the outdoor swimming pool. Unaware of the danger, I was playing inside one of these happily. I remember him having to hold onto me with one arm as he clung on with the other, both of us being bashed against the rocks by the waves. I was about seven or eight years of age.

It was murder when we got back. Mam was still soaking up the sun. She flounced off in her bathing costume, a towel over her shoulder. Dad sat on the slope from the lifeboat station, looking miserable. I didn't know how to cheer him up so I found a tiny crab in a rock pool and took it to him. *This will make him happy*, I thought. After taking the crab from me, he picked an empty corned beef tin from a wire bin and placed the creature inside, nipping the edges tightly shut. He then walked slowly down to the edge of the sea, dug a hole and covered over the tin with sand. I continually attempted to dig it up, but each time he prevented me.

'Leave it, it's trapped, like me!' he told me.

Soon, the tide washed over and I could no longer tell where it was.

CHAPTER TWO

Betting, Break-ups and Blattas

I blamed myself for the death of the crab, but it wasn't until many years later that Dad was diagnosed with Asperger syndrome. Until then, everyone thought at best, he was a loner or simply childish, at worst, that he was rude and cold. We would go off to Elswick Park together and roll down the hill, which was great fun, but when I got tired, he would go down another few times on his own. When I was given my first two-wheeler bike, he took me to the park to practise riding it. There were stabilisers on the wheels so it was quite easy for the first couple of months until he took them off. He held onto the seat and ran alongside as I continually looked back to make sure that he was still there. Then, one day, he had let go and I was riding on my own.

Of course, because of my new-found confidence, I was

pedalling back and forth along my stretch of the lane, but one day, I strayed into the other half and the bike was taken from me. Streets and back lanes were very territorial places in those days and you could be chased or have your possessions confiscated. Luckily for me, the lad rode around on it for a few revolutions and then gave it back. Afterwards, I concentrated on riding in the opposite direction and turned the corner onto St John's Road, where a sharp dip wasn't allowed for. My feet slipped from the pedals as the bike picked up speed and the chain fell off the spokes. No brakes! The corner of Hannah Street was right in my path. As my backside rose from the saddle, I went headfirst into the wall. Only half of my face bore the impact and it immediately puffed up purple in colour. For weeks I looked like the Elephant Man. The bruises attracted attention and people commented on the colour as they changed from purple and then blue to yellow and brown.

Ryton Park and Leazes Park were regulars for us as we could take our fishing nets to catch minnows. We would put them in jam jars, but they rarely lasted more than a few days. A pal of mine, Nicky, lived a few doors away and we played together in the lane. I asked if we could take him with us to Ryton Park one Sunday and his mother agreed. We caught the bus along Scotswood Road over the Chain Bridge and settled ourselves at the river's edge. Now, I have never been enamoured by spiders, but this day, my dad caught one and proceeded to dangle it in front of me. It was then that I discovered that Nicky was scared of them too. We retreated into the river, away from Dad's taunting. He thought it a huge joke, but this only reinforced my fear. (Today, I have a gun-like catcher with fibres on one end so I can capture spiders humanely and release them into the garden.)

Dad once snapped a seeding plant from a bush and asked me to hold it in my hand. This I did and a tiny explosion erupted inside my closed grip. I was temporarily shocked by this, but quickly recovered and asked if he could find another. This wasn't of interest to him, but I soon learned that if I could pretend that I enjoyed an experience, it wouldn't happen again. Pity I didn't twig before the spider incident!

I can't remember ever wanting a farm set, but Dad made one for me anyway. I distinctly recall longing for a dolls' house, but instead I was taken to Fenwick, a large department store in Newcastle, to buy an animal from the toy floor once a week. A duck, or horse, maybe a pig, but only one until I had enough to populate the yard. Dad fixed short fencing around the circumference of a large piece of board: it had a little gate which tied to the post with a leather loop. He created the pigsty, stable and cottage from plywood and there was even a piece of mirror surrounded by fake grass. I played with it occasionally, but eventually swapped it for some books from a lad in my class.

Dad also enjoyed board games, so we played Snakes and Ladders. When we became bored, we went up a snake and down a ladder. Card games were popular too and Three-card Brag was his favourite. Ludo was a source of irritation as the cardboard stand which held the cup was always collapsing when I pressed a counter intending it to go into the cup. Dad bought a broom shank and sawed it into little discs, painted half of them black and the other half white. He spent an age plotting and drawing squares onto a smaller board. These were also painted black and white, and so we had a draughts game. This was my favourite.

One day, Dad came home with a blue budgie in a cage and put it on a stand in the sitting room. He said it was going to be called Johnny. The bird was allowed to fly freely around the room, leaving its little parcels everywhere, but it was easy enough to chisel them off once they went solid. Mam wasn't exactly house-proud, she was more concerned with the budgie interrupting her lounge-about times by interacting with her mule slippers. After his arrival we noticed that the coleus plant was looking a little bedraggled and Johnny was the culprit. That Christmas, I spent night after night making decorations with crepe paper cut into strips to make chains. There were no such things as glue sticks back then so wallpaper paste was employed, which was very messy. When the chains were dry, Dad fixed them in a circle from the ceiling rose and led each one to the outer edges of the ceiling, which created a lovely web of colour. Johnny, however, looked on this as a playground and jumped from one to the other and snapped each one. Dad just left the room and Mam used the ladders to try and fix them in her fashion – it looked rubbish.

But this bird was the light of Dad's life: it sat on his finger and repeated everything he said, didn't answer back and was all he wanted, the budgie equivalent of a Stepford wife. Mam wasn't so keen as this Johnny was a sex addict. Back then, she wore pink Maribou-covered mules and if she sat with her feet on the pouffe, Johnny liked nothing better than to have a quick shag on the fur. She used to kick her foot up. He would fly off then but immediately clamped back on – he wasn't about to give up that easily! I quite liked him: he was fun when I propped a mirror up against a box. He chirruped, bobbed and bashed his beak against the glass, then went for a peek behind the mirror as if wondering where the real bird was – probably to pin that down as well.

Dad would sit in his armchair teaching his new pal how to speak: 'Johnny's a pretty bird', 'Johnny likes his seed', etc, while Mam gave him withering looks and tried to be out of the house as much as possible.

I even wrote a poem about Johnny while I was at South Benwell School:

> *I have a little bird and his name is Johnny*
> *I must admit he is rather bonnie.*
> *His nose is yellow, his eyes are blue*
> *He has a little beak that the seed goes through.*

I must credit Mam with the last line. As I read the first few lines to her and said that I couldn't think of how to end the poem, she came up with it.

Unfortunately, after Dad had taught his pet an extensive repertoire and spoken to the bird more than anyone else, there was to be a tragedy. I was in a hurry one day to get out to play with my friends and as I slammed the kitchen door, Johnny was on his way to fly through. I just about decapitated Dad's little pal. He was in his armchair at the time and when he saw this happen, he was heartbroken. Sobbingly uncontrollably, he held Johnny lovingly in his hand. I was the demon child for a week, until he bought a new bird.

Ronnie joined our family and was given the same attention as his predecessor, but he wasn't to last long either. This time it wasn't my fault – Dad left the kitchen door open while fetching in a shovelful of coal for the fire and he escaped, with Dad running after him across the road, oblivious to traffic. The bird made it over the high wall into the graveyard and was never seen again. We didn't have another bird in the house after that and the cage was given away to some other budgie fancier.

I went along to Scotswood Road swimming pool on my own during Dad's period of mourning. It was a really dilapidated old place with chipped tiles and two old pools, one of them wasn't used, and a foot of stagnating water slimed about at the deep end. There was a communal laundry in the building and around the upper floor we could see the coal miners, pitch-black with soot, paying for a cubicle to have a hot bath after a shift, as none of them had a tub at home.

One day, during the six weeks' summer holiday, the pool was packed with children of all ages. All I remember is the feeling that someone from behind was carrying me towards the deep end. When I looked around, it was a lad a little older than me who I didn't know. He dropped me and swam away. As I began to sink, there was so much noise. No one noticed as I struggled to stay afloat. I sank further down and the most beautiful rainbow colours began to gently and peacefully float all around, until someone dragged me to the surface. The pain really kicked in then as I struggled for breath and was pulled to the side of the pool. Once I'd regained my breath, the pool attendants got back to their jobs and I'd forgotten all about it by the time I got home. I wasn't given swimming lessons until much later when I attended secondary school.

So, me and Dad returned to our usual haunts of the park and Whitley Bay. My brother David was born when I was much older and he was taken to the same places. He later summed it up:

'At first, I thought it was great to be going out, but when I wanted to go somewhere different, he refused and went to his favourite haunts without me.'

We also compared notes on story time. There wasn't a children's book in the house, only Dad's *Reader's Digest* magazines, Charles Atlas fitness routines and a couple of medical books, so he made up his own. In *Foxy and the Chickens*, the chickens never escaped, Foxy always managed to get past the farmer, tear the wire, break down the door to the hen house and they all 'had their chips'.

Another memory we shared was that Dad had a nickname for us: I was 'Fatty Buster' and my brother David was 'Fatty Lumper'. Dad always had a curious dislike of overweight people and it was very uncomfortable to be around him when a stout person came into his orbit. Even the names of local villages were changed to become the butt of his jokes. As we passed through Percy Main railway station on the way to the coast he always shouted out, 'We are now passing the Porky Man!'

One winter, we were walking along Elswick Road. It was very icy and a large man slipped and thudded onto the path. No thought was given to helping the poor soul up.

'See that? That's because he's fat, he wouldn't have gone over if he had been slim!'

The winters in Benwell were usually severe, but none more so than when the snow of 1963 arrived. As the homes had no central heating, snow blankets a foot thick covered the rooftops. From this, huge icicles up to a couple of feet long spiked down. I was very aware of those big buggers staring down at me as I knocked on a friend's door.

'Are yi comin' oot ter play?'

'Nah, me Mam says the snow's too bad.' (Other parents seemed to show more concern for the effects of adverse weather conditions than mine. I was never expected to ask their permission to go out, or agree what time to be back. I was generally the last one playing out in the dark whilst others were long since by the fire.)

Sometimes the slam of the door was enough to send the whole lot thundering down. But it wasn't so bad then as I had a free ice lolly, even though it tasted of soot. Of course, if my friend had been allowed out, we could have had a sword fight, an icicle each as our weapons, or even a game of snowball fights. Also, if a bucket of water had frozen solid, it could be released from its galvanised steel base to be smashed into smithereens. Our hands would be numb from the cold.

As I made my way back home, I walked through the trenches of snow which had been dug out by all of the neighbours – they were so high, I couldn't see over the top. This was in no way a traditional white snowy scene from the Christmas cards as soot covered the surface. I always found it very pleasing to press my foot through to reveal the pristine white glow beneath.

Lads could be seen rolling snow into a giant ball from Buddle Road towards Frank Street. When it was around eight feet tall, it would be set loose down one of the steep streets. What a sight to behold as it picked up more height as it went. Heaven help anyone who got in the way!

Back home, it was as cold inside as out and the net curtains stuck to the glass on the windows. I once got my tongue stuck as I tried to lick the snowflake patterns. Trying to shout 'Mam' for help without the use of your tongue to pronounce a word came out as 'AAA'. But the most exciting thing was if my mother forgot to bring the washing in and it came in frozen solid. I wondered what would have happened if I crashed a jumper against the wall, would it have just melted the ice or would the garment have snapped in two? Of course, I was never allowed to find out.

A bucket was kept next to the back door so that ash could be sprinkled to guide the way to the outside toilet. Pipes were always bursting so they would be wrapped in old rags to keep them warm – not a pretty sight. The seat would be covered in ice, so unless you wanted to slide about mid-pee, the surface needed to be scraped off. In summer, however, the danger was sitting on the woodworm holes: the preparation to kill them was very smelly indeed and this would be transferred to the backs of your legs. I discovered that if I banged on the seat with my fist, little worms would pop their heads out and then I was waiting with a pin to try and stick one. Nowadays, there is a fairground game with lots of holes on a huge board. Once money has been paid, random worm heads pop up and the skill of the game is to bash as many as you can with a hammer. I often wonder if the person who invented this entertainment also used a toilet seat with woodworm as a kid.

* * *

Many of the flats and houses in the West End had long since been deemed unfit for human habitation, but landlords were still able to rent out to folks who couldn't afford a better place. A five-year-old lad called Larry had a younger brother of three, who was playing in the lane after Sunday dinner. He had the wishbone from the chicken and Larry wanted it too so he chased him. The little lad bumped into a backyard wall, the whole lot came tumbling down and killed him. Later, when the police arrived, they knocked down fifteen walls in the lane using a wooden clothes prop. The walls weren't repaired, and the dwellings remained occupied with the backyards exposed to the lane. Demolition of the properties didn't commence until some years later.

But playing outdoors in all weathers was all we did. I would check if anyone else was willing to brave the elements. I took my sledge which Dad had made, materials courtesy of the workplace, steel runners included. To find a street where the housewives hadn't emptied ash was a task. This was done as there was no way delivery wagons could attempt those steep streets without it in such weather. One did venture forth and it happened to be a wines and spirits lorry. The vehicle skidded then fell over, bottles were everywhere, and so too were the neighbours. There were reports of a good festive season that year.

Buses had an awful time getting through and when they did, we couldn't see the numbers on the front as they had been bleached out by the snow. But even worse was the dreaded New Year's Eve as my folks watched *The White Heather Club* with Andy Stewart dressed in his kilt. He sang 'Mairi's Wedding' or 'A Scottish Soldier' as he hopped from one muscle-bound leg to the other, a little raise of his shoulder in time with the music. Though probably only in his twenties, to me he seemed ancient. Scenery consisted of a false log lying on the floor, on which Andy perched a foot every now and then to give the impression that there was some action going on. The background was usually a painted mountain greenery effect to give the illusion that the show was set outdoors. The women pranced about in flouncy cotton dresses even though it was the middle of winter. They held onto the edges of their skirts and curtsied daintily at the close of each dance, then they were off again, white high heels, pearls and tatted [backcombed] hairstyles which before hair lacquer they used sugar and water to hold in place. Although I must admit that I did enjoy singing along with Donald 'Where's Yer Troosers?' and Scottish singing star Moira Anderson appearing in her frock, I couldn't wait for them to sing 'Auld Lang Syne' and for the Epilogue to kick in. That was boring too, but it meant my suffering would be over soon. Dad insisted we stood for the National Anthem, which was a sign that the little white dot in the centre of the box was about to appear. Then at last, it was off to bed.

* * *

My brother David was born too late to visit Gateshead as I'd known it – all the old buildings had been demolished by then – but Mam continued to seek refuge from Dad with her sister Ellen, who lived in Low Fell. She'd stay there for a week, two or six, depending on how she felt at the time. She took on a new job at Bowers Restaurant in town as a dish washer. I called in the odd time to see her and was fascinated by the waitresses. They carried four dinners in each hand, an edge of the plates between each digit, dropping them onto various tables on their way past. Fish and chips, pie and mash, egg and chips… These women had muscles! It was an embarrassment for Mam at Christmas as the women were bringing in jewellery, clothes and perfume to show off. She didn't receive presents from Dad as he didn't think it was necessary to give gifts, so she usually told them she got nighties, a dressing gown and some slippers. Stuff they wouldn't ask to see. He lacked empathy, and didn't really understand that someone would gain pleasure from receiving presents. Why waste money? Mam always bought for him, but this was just to keep up appearances so that she didn't have to come up with another lie for her workmates.

There were free tickets dished out to restaurant staff from performers at the nearby Empire Theatre, who called in for fish and chips. I saw *A Midsummer Night's Dream* there and put my sixpence in the slot to use the binoculars. We also saw pantomimes starring the male tenor David Whitfield and puppet shows there. Two policemen used to call in for coffee at the restaurant and one of them fancied Mam – she would chat to him in her break in Nun's Lane. This was the first time that she admitted to herself that she wanted to leave Dad, but it never actually came to that.

During the school holidays if I wasn't with a neighbour until my parents finished work, then I would spend the whole six weeks at my grandparents' home in Gateshead. My first memory of that house was when I was about fifteen months old and it was the day of HM Queen Elizabeth II's Coronation, 2 June 1953. The dining-room table had been cleared except for the plum velour cloth. My aunt and uncles bought *The Coronation Cut-Out Story Book* and painstakingly cut out every horse, guardsman, Beefeater and the golden coach with Her Majesty inside. The palace scene was in the background and they waited patiently for the proceedings to be transmitted via radio ('the wireless') – usually Rediffusion, who distributed TV and radio signals. We paid weekly for this service and the dial was fitted on the windowsill behind the curtain, only around three channels from what I remember. I was dying to get my hands on the little horses, but the adults kept me well back while they paraded their cardboard cut-outs across the table as the ceremony was relayed across the airwaves.

* * *

Gateshead city centre was the poor relation to Newcastle. We had libraries, art galleries and some cafés, but they did have Saltwell Park. Mam walked me along Scotswood Road, across Redheugh Bridge and down Askew Road to Fleming Street, where my grandparents lived. On the way over the bridge we looked down towards the Tyne, a very dirty river in the fifties and sixties – rats ran everywhere along the Quayside. Mam told me there were tales of the River Girls, who were very wicked:

'And, if you don't behave at your granny's, they will come and get you to take you down there!'

Of course, I didn't believe a word of it. When I was about four years old at Granny's, I picked up an empty milk bottle and began tottering down the stone steps into the yard, tumbled and fell onto the broken glass, which pierced my arm. Then they all took notice. Les held me, while Willy fetched a pair of tweezers from the first aid box. When he attempted to pick the glass out, my screams were enough to convince them to seek the skill of a doctor.

Another time Mam dropped me off – she was popping up to the stores and the only person at home was Willy. He was trimming the white hairs from his quiff in front of a mirror set up in front of a box of cereal. Satisfied he had removed any evidence of ageing, he got himself cosy in the armchair and fell fast asleep. When Mam came back, I was minus a fringe! It seemed like a good idea to copy what I had just witnessed.

Unfortunately, I have a really high forehead and looked like Max Wall.

* * *

The year 1962 was the centenary of the Blaydon Races and there were plans for mass celebrations along Scotswood Road, where the first race was held in 1862. Every Newcastle lad and lass knows the words to the song, 'The Blaydon Races':

> *Aa went to Blaydon Races*
> *'twas on the ninth of June*
> *Eighteen hundred and sixty-two*
> *on a summer's afternoon.*
> *Aa took the bus from Balmbra's*
> *And she was heavy laden*
> *Away we went alang Collingwood Street*
> *That's on the road to Blaydon.*
> *[Chorus]*
> *Ah me lads, you should a seen us gannin'*
> *We passed the folks alang the road*
> *Just as they were stannin'*
> *There was lots of lads and lasses there*
> *Aal with smilin' faces*
> *Gannin' alang the Scotswood Road*
> *To see the Blaydon Races.*
> *We flew past Armstrong's factory*
> *And up to the Robin Adair*
> *Just gannin' doon to the railway bridge*

The bus wheel flew off there
The lasses lost their crinolines off
And the veils that hide their faces
Aa got two black eyes and a broken nose
The day we went to Blaydon.

(And more verses describing local characters Coffy Johnny, Geordie Ridley, Jackie Brown, Doctor Gibbs, and landmarks – Chain Bridge and The Mechanics Hall.)

Only I missed the whole thing, didn't I? I was at my grandparents', the Romes, in Gateshead. Friends told me of the street parties: all the chairs from folks' homes were taken outdoors and tables set up with food. Each side of the Scotswood Road, from the town to the bridge over to Blaydon, was thronged with the whole community. There were bands, processions on flatbed lorries from all of the industries along the Tyne, costumes, customised vehicles and music. It all began at Balmbra's Music Hall, which had been in business for over a century. The Elswick Harriers ran, brass bands played. I saw photographs of the fabulous wagons decorated to advertise their businesses; there was a huge bottle of Guinness, W & H.O. Wills float had a huge filter-tipped cigarette aboard, there were people dressed in period clothing, top hats, crinolines, Scottish dancers, a vintage car rally, penny-farthing bikes and the City Council Pipe Band and much more. I missed the whole lot as neither of my parents thought that I might like to be there to be part of a once-in-a-century event.

* * *

Most houses on both sides of the river, Newcastle and Gateshead, were decorated in the same battleship grey, green or brown paint, courtesy of the shipyards. This made rooms and stairways very dark, spooky places; my imagination always went into overdrive as I climbed the stairs. Fleming Street was only half electric lighting and half gas, which meant mantle fittings. Sometimes I would be on my way up there and the mantle would pop, sending hissing flames shooting out. I couldn't wait to get into the sitting room, where the electric light bulb glowed continuously. My grandparents had a dog called Max, who would throw his head back and howl in response to any loud noise, such as lightning or a car backfiring. He hid under the table during Guy Fawkes night. They also kept a cat, who Max was afraid of as well.

Grandad Rome was a fireman and a boxer. He won cups for fighting and would regularly travel down to Carlisle to take part in matches. Although a tall strong bloke, he made a hasty retreat one evening on his return from the Donnie, a local pub. He witnessed two men stealing spirits from a local shop, one was passing the bottles to the other through a broken pane of glass. Grandad noticed a policeman on the corner so he approached him.

'Hey, there are two blokes stealing booze up there.'

'Get lost, mate, before I nick you for it!' he was told. The policeman was their lookout and doubtless received a bottle or two for his trouble.

Granny didn't work – she said that it was enough to do the washing with a poss-tub and mangle for a daughter and three sons still living at home in their twenties. Ellen was the youngest and she worked at Osram Lamps, a factory on the Team Valley Trading Estate, which made miniature and high-wattage incandescent and decorative candle types of lamp. Previously, she had worked for Rowntree's and used to have allowances of Smarties and such-like – I was gutted when she changed jobs. She used to take me to Saltwell Park, where there was a boating lake and a lovely museum which looked like a fairy-tale castle, with ribbons flowing from the steeples. We never went inside – Ellen and her sister Lillian were too busy posing past the lads. Eventually Ellen gained a long-term boyfriend called Pete, who was very good-looking, with a Teddy Boy quiff. He wore a suit and took her dancing. He walked her home and stood at the front door, calling her 'Chick' – I used to sit on the landing, listening. When she was going out, Ellen wore starched slips which really stood out and she had to hold the front of the hem when she sat down as the whole ensemble hooped up like a TV aerial.

Pete and Ellen soon became closer and were seeing each other every night. When Ellen became pregnant, my mam and an aunt arranged a meeting with Pete's parents to lay down the law: either he married her or he wouldn't see her again. But this wasn't an issue as the pair were planning that very thing anyway. They moved into the front room in Fleming Street until they got their own place and Jacqueline was born soon after, followed by their son Michael (they were still together until Ellen died in her seventies, but Jacqueline tragically died of a brain haemorrhage in her twenties).

Willy was Granny's eldest son. He liked betting on the dogs and horses and doing the Football Pools. Also, dancing in the house – he never went to ballrooms, but would stride from one side of the room to the other, head held way back, trailing the side of his shoe before turning. Willy would shout at the radiogram when the score draws came on, Littlewoods Pools sheet in hand. After each result,

'Ah, nah, man!'

'Dunfermline 0… Charlton Athletic…'

'Nil, man, c'mon, man, Niiiiiiiiil!'

'Charlton Athletic 2.'

'Ah, bloody hell!'

Around this time Ellen had discovered Cliff Richard. If he was on TV, she would crouch down about a quarter of an inch in front of the screen, screaming something about movin' and groovin'.

'Cliiiiiiif, Cliiiiiiif, isn't he gorgeous?'

To which the others would shout:

'We don't know as none of us can see what he looks like!'

'We can't even hear him!'

Or even:

'Get out of the way, man!'

One day, there were kittens, five of them, and Ellen was only allowed to keep one. For about two hours she picked the tabby up and eventually said, 'This one!', breaking her heart for the others. And then, 'No, this one,' picking up the ginger one. Before, 'Ah, but can't we keep them all, please?'

'No, only one,' she was told in no uncertain terms.

Time after time, she eventually picked little ginger, knowing all too well that the others would be drowned in a bucket. This was the cruel practice back then – every cat-owning family did this, vets weren't heard of. The poor cats didn't stand a chance, but the kids would often snaffle some stray to put a dress on it and pin it down in their dolls' pram.

Willy worked for Sowerby's Glassworks in Gateshead. He was a glass blower and very skilled at his job. All of our relatives owned something he had created – vases, bowls, dressing table sets, candlesticks, etc. The colours were beautiful: amber, swirly mauve and cream, pink and clear glass. Whether all of these items were officially supposed to be there, we didn't ask. But eventually Willy's gambling habits got the better of him and he left work and went on the dole, betting and gambling more than ever.

Les was the middle brother and had been a soldier in the army, serving in Egypt and Singapore; he used to bring me lovely silk Suzie Wong-style pyjamas. On his return, he secured a position at Huwoods Mining Machinery, also on Team Valley.

John, the youngest, worked at the paper mill, but I do remember that he also put the odd bet on the horses. There were arguments with Willy when the newspaper was delivered:

'I'm bringing money into this house while you sit on your fat arse all day, it's mine first!'

Willy was six-foot tall, while John was only around five-foot four so they would be just like the cartoon characters in a comic, the big 'un holding the forehead of the little 'un while he was trying to take a swing at his taller opponent. Nobody took any notice of this. Eventually there would be a winner and grumpiness, but it was soon forgotten.

John was about to be married to a beautiful woman called Nora. I went to Shepherd's, a department store which sold all sorts in the centre of Gateshead, with Ellen and Granny. The shop had its own currency, a kind of tokens system. I recall Granny trying on a few suits, which she called 'costumes', and one of them had diamanté buttons. I tried all ways to convince her to buy it, just for the buttons. The family kept a buttons box containing all of the buttons from various items of clothing, which had become tatty and subsequently thrown out. In time, the costume would suffer the same fate and I would be the proud owner of the offcuts. I was gutted when she chose a different outfit.

'No, it's too dear.'

I was to be a bridesmaid, along with another little girl, who I presume was a relative of Nora's. We were only about five years old, but I thought we looked better than the bride. Our dresses were cream satin with matching furry boleros and silver sandals. The reception was held at the top of the street above the Co-op. There weren't many people there and I was sitting next to a very jolly man, who kept me constantly entertained by drawing on the tablecloth. One of the aunts didn't seem to like him, though.

'Don't talk to him, he's horrible,' she said.

But I was having none of this – I thought he was a great laugh.

'Look under the table,' she said. 'Look at the mess he's made.'

This man had been eating sandwiches from the buffet and chucking the crusts under the table.

In spite of all of these goings-on, the happy couple left for their honeymoon. But all was not as it seemed: John was working all hours and she gave money to her parents for their visits to the local alehouse. The marriage didn't last long and he was devastated and wound up back home. When I stayed there I slept between two armchairs, so after John had been drowning his sorrows in the pub, he used to sit at the table, pontificating. The next day, after one particular evening out, I mentioned to him that he had spoken about marriage.

'I didn't tell you anything, did I?' He looked shocked.

'No, just that marriage didn't work. You were singing.'

'Thank God for that!'

'John,' I asked, 'that song, "Love and marriage goes together like a horse and carriage?", is it a tender trap?'

'It certainly is,' he replied.

'Well, why does it say you can't have one without the other?'

'Oh, never mind.'

* * *

My best pal in Fleming Street was Sandra, who lived with her gran and mam in a downstairs flat. She was constantly in tears because of kids shouting after her, 'You get free school dinners cos you've got no dad!' Her poor mam did all she could to comfort her, but the damage was done, she cried for a while and then we went into her bedroom. There was a huge bed to which you would need a block and tackle (a system of pulleys) to climb up to. Sandra explained to me that she was going to turn the light off, then quickly switch it back on again, while I was to stare at the floor. When the room lit up again after about half a minute, the floor was covered in cockroaches (which were known to us as 'blattas'). They immediately dashed for cover, leaving the floor clear again. This was the most horrific sight: how could she sleep in that room knowing as soon as it was dark, the little bleeders would be everywhere?

'They aren't from our place,' she said firmly, 'they're from the family upstairs – they burrow through the plaster to get in here.'

Next day, she asked if I would like to meet the neighbours. The image of what I saw there has never left me: no carpet on the stairs and no painted walls. The sitting room had no carpet or lino, only bare floorboards, with one big table in the centre of the room and two chairs (I had heard of people burning the furniture when it got cold if they couldn't afford coal). The mother was cooking soup in a large tin pan on the stove. The children and their parents all looked grey – their clothing, skin, everything about them, grey. The mother took the pan from the heat, placed it on the table and used a ladle to pour a spoonful into each bowl, but the soup looked little more than grey water. But this lady asked me and Sandra if we would like some. We declined, as it would have meant there was less for their poor children. Sandra said that the man had lost his job and the family were struggling. At one end of the table were towers of coins. She explained that they were for the gas man from the meter and when he collected the money, the family would be given a small dividend. They were waiting and depending on this meagre handout. I learned a lesson that day in kindness and sharing – and the injustice of hard-working men who were reduced to this when work fell off.

Sandra took me to the Team Valley Trading Estate one day, where all the factories were. I learned from her how to go on.

'We stand out the back of the bakery and look in. Someone always comes to the door and gives me a cake or a pie.'

True to her word, this actually happened. As we walked along to the next place, which prepared cardboard packaging, we came away with some little boxes to play with. Further along towards the river, Sandra showed me the River Team – there were huge industrial wheels and cogs no longer in use, abandoned. This was very scary to me as she was climbing on things and I could see the oily water below so we left. Walking back to an office building, there was a skip outside, where we found carbon paper and lots of sheets of ordinary paper.

'This will be great for playing offices.'

We gathered armfuls of the stuff and then noticed two men wearing business suits were staring at us:

'Bloody scavengers!'

Sandra's school was across the other side of the High Street. It was open throughout the six weeks in summer for children from one-parent families or whose fathers were out of work – at least they would have one hot dinner a day. She took me there one day and the sight of those poor children, well down on their luck, saddened me. I felt so guilty taking food that day when both of my parents were working. I never went back.

There was an old shop on the corner of that street and the owner let the upstairs room out to a Spiritualist group.

'They will all be sitting around a table calling for the spirits to tell them stuff,' Sandra said.

So, we went to the foot of the stairs and shouted, 'Wooooooo, hooooooo!' up there and then ran away.

Up and down every street, the women would pull sash windows up and lean on windowsills to look out the window up and down the street – we called it 'Tooting on the neighbours'. Mrs Patterson lived opposite my granny and she would pull a chair up and sit smoking as she 'tooted'. No wonder gossip got around. A new coffee had just been introduced and the advert featured a drum – '*Boom bang-a-bang, Boom bang-a-bang, Patterson's Instant Coffee!*' It was great fun for me and Sandra, singing this refrain with the window open, but with us hiding on the floor.

Les would say, 'Little things amuse little minds,' then walk out.

I used to invite a couple of lasses to sit in the front bedroom, where we told stories, but they always preferred mine from Benwell. Like the time when two lads went into a disused coal mine in Elswick and were missing for a week before they were found dead. Nobody knew they were there – they had gone in through the old wheelhouse with candles, matches, a pickaxe and a sack, the idea being to take some coal and sell it round the doors. Of course, the matches went out and they became confused in the dark, going deeper and deeper inside. A man I know called Matty who used to work tarring along Scotswood Road said that he worked for a company called Jobling Purser at the time, which was next door. He had heard tapping sounds and it made him shudder as he imagined it was ghosts of the lads, trying to find their way out.

They weren't so keen when I told them of Dad's brother George, a gunner for the Northumberland Fusiliers. He came back from France and couldn't come to terms with what he had witnessed, so he blew his brains out with a shotgun in Granny's house, where they lived in Elswick at the time. Dad had to sweep up the pieces of bone before she got home, but there was blood everywhere. Being born so close to the end of wartime, it was inconceivable to imagine the suffering of women, like my grandmother, who lost their sons in such terrible circumstances, or the lads who just went missing and were never heard of again.

I remember Dad was looking through the cardboard box on one occasion when he found a little green silk handkerchief, which he said Granny had sent him with a pound note on his twenty-first when he was in service. He admitted that he never read any of her letters.

Because Benwell, Elswick and Scotswood were going through stages of demolition, there were dangers all around: disused pits, breakers' yards, old houses with no doors on and crumbling hearths. When industry was thriving on Tyneside all of the factories and ammunitions shops were fully manned, but industries were in decline. Now, there were holes in fencing and children saw these places as adventure playgrounds. The girls listened, enthralled, as I told how me and my pals climbed inside derelict buildings and scaled the walls around holes in the floor. I told them the story of how we dared each other to step inside the old church with its huge wooden, iron-studded doors hanging from their hinges. I wrapped all of this in bravery, but that day we ventured inside the old church is one I will never forget. The gaping hole in the floorboards flooded with water… Hairs stand up on the back of my neck when I think of it, but I gained kudos for that one.

Me and Sandra used to enjoy listening to the Salvation Army playing and singing in a circle right in the middle of the street on Sundays. But this didn't please the working men:

'The only bloody day in the week we have the chance of a lie-in and them buggers turn up!'

Of course, the Sally Army did so much for families in the area so nobody really minded that much. There was also a mission on Vine Street, just off the High Street, which Sandra took me to. She said that if we learned the names of all of the Books in the Bible, we would be given one of our own. My mam used to say, 'You would go anywhere for a little apple,' which was her way of saying I was up for anything free. We sat down in the hall and everyone began to sing,

Will you come to the mission, will you come?
Bring your own cup of tea and a bun.

We played games and had a good time, but then the reciting was to begin in earnest. I was able to remember: Genesis, Exodus, Leviticus, Numbers, Deuteronomy, Joshua, Judges, Ruth. First second Samuel, First second Kings.

I got fed up and packed it in, so I didn't get a Bible – Sandra did, though. Even to this day, in my sixty-sixth year, if anyone mentions the word 'Bible', I'm away at a gallop up until Kings. Recently, I was talking to someone who remembered the lady who ran the mission, Winifred Laver. She came from a well-to-do family in the South and had worked in a hospital, becoming a nurse and then a nun. When a position came up in Gateshead, she applied and got the job. At the time Gateshead had the worst record for TB and unemployment. Her folks were horrified and the family doctor said that if she went there, she would be dead within a year.

Sister Winifred held surgeries for families who couldn't afford doctors' bills. One little lad was at her surgery, suffering from a sore leg. Winifred applied a bread poultice and when he got outside, he ate the poultice – times were hard. She took children on trips to the seaside, fund-raised and gave food to needy families. Breakfasts were given to those who attended church on Sundays, so the congregation swelled during her ministry. She retired when she was ninety and died at the age of ninety-two. It was said that over four hundred people from all over the world came into contact with her as children wrote to speak of her kindness. I suddenly realised that she was probably there when I was attempting to get my hands on something for nothing.

Early one Sunday morning, as usual the sound of the Salvation Army belting out their music woke folks up for church. Around then it was also a common sight to see a priest at some kid's front door – the child would escape from the back door only to be captured by another Man of the Cloth and taken off to attend Mass.

As I wasn't from the area, this didn't apply to me. The lane was where anyone who escaped the Sunday morning ritual would congregate. A baby was crying in its pram, so I went up the path through the backyard.

'Your baby's crying.'

'Oh, thank you,' said the father, 'I'm coming out now.'

I followed him to the pram.

'I haven't got a brother or sister.'

'Well, you can have her for two bob.'

I raced back to Granny's.

'Please can I have two shillings to buy a baby?'

'What are you on about?'

'A man in the lane is selling a baby for two shillings and I can have her!'

'Go away with you! He's only joking, man.'

'No, he's not. He said, really.'

I was fizzing that they wouldn't believe me – they were wrong, he was going to sell her. Back in the lane, I waited until the dad came back out.

'They wouldn't give me the money, so I can't buy her just now.'

'Just as well,' he said. 'She's not for sale any longer.'

Back indoors and in a huff, I was furious with the baby's father but didn't tell my relatives that they were right.

* * *

The betting shop was also on the High Street and one day, Les, John and Willy were listening to the horse racing on the wireless. Crouched around the marble-effect tiled fireplace, they pounded their fists on it as the race gained pace.

'Go down to the bakery and get us eight pies, here's the money.'

I decided to take my bike with me – I could hang the carrier bag across the handlebars on the way back. Once I had paid for the pies, the assistant put them on the counter wrapped individually in tissue paper (they had no carrier bags). So, I balanced each pie, one on top of the other, on the saddle of my bike and painstakingly wheeled it up the road. I had got as far as the top of the street when the front wheel kinked on a stone and every pie hit the deck. Hurtling into the room, I was in floods of tears. Nothing was said except:

'Don't take the bike this time.'

And I was given a shopping bag.

If someone strayed into crime or let themselves go regarding their appearance, people would say, 'She's gone to the dogs' or 'They've gone to the dogs' so of course when my Uncle Willy was going to the hounds track on the Teams to watch the race, I imagined he was really far gone.

In the kitchen there was a dingy pantry with a tiny window, but they never kept anything in there except tins of paint. But the cupboard in the sitting room had plaster walls, which were always painted white. Empty pop bottles were kept in there and I enjoyed filling them to different levels to play a tune using an old metal spoon. While I was in there with the door open, I noticed a piece of flat wood with a piece of cheese on it.

'What's this?' I said, holding it aloft.

'Jesus, give that here!' said Grandad. 'It's a mousetrap and if you put your finger in there, you'll know about it!'

Grown-ups were always saying things that didn't make sense.

My cousin Ellen 'knew about it' one day when she was helping to do the washing. Granny wasn't feeling well so Ellen took over. Pushing the sheets through a huge iron mangle with wooden rollers, she picked up wodges of the soaking cotton to feed it through.

'Mind your fingers!' came the advice from the sitting room.

Too late, the tips of her fingers were crunched and Willy came rushing through to pull the rollers apart. The men had to finish off after that.

It turned out Granny was far worse than anyone expected: she had stomach cancer, and one day she was taken away on a stretcher into an ambulance, with Ellen hanging onto the side of it, screaming. Granny wouldn't be coming back home. She died in hospital. The times were changing and I was about to be given the key to the front door at home, so not many visits to the Romes were on the cards afterwards.

When I returned home, I thought of Granny, our days at the beach and the times she and Mam took me to the cinema. Some of the films weren't to my liking – *Oklahoma!*, for example. Jud Fry terrified me and I started to cry. But Mam wasn't in the mood to interrupt her film simply because I was being a wimp,

'Just put your head on my knee.'

Granny had been willing to leave, but was persuaded otherwise.

Another time we went to see a scary film about prehistoric monsters and I wasn't about to be pacified and screamed the place down, so we were forced to vacate the premises. I wrote a letter to Granny telling her how much I missed her and if she could read it, she would know. How I loved to see her wearing her fox fur stole with its little black nose and beady eyes, how it appeared to be biting its own tail when she clipped it on. I placed the letter on the middle of the sash window, where it stayed for weeks (Mam wasn't bothered about how clean the windows were as she was finding entertainment elsewhere).

A few years later, Grandad Rome died. I was in the room when it happened. He put a plate of dinner down on the table, staggered to the wall, pressed his hands against it in an attempt to steady himself, careered off again into the chair, which he made a grab for, but instead fell to the floor. I don't remember what happened next as I was removed from the room. In those days adults didn't speak to children or tell them what was happening so they formed their own thoughts and usually came to the wrong conclusions. A day or so later, I walked into the back bedroom and there he was, stone-cold white and wrapped in a sheet of the same colour, lying on a board between the backs of two dining chairs. The iron fireplace was like a wind tunnel, leading to the open elements – it sounded as if someone was howling all around me.

* * *

My first day at South Benwell Primary School did not go well. A classmate was celebrating a birthday and it was the usual practice in Class 1 for the teacher to celebrate by way of using a wooden cake. The birthday girl or boy would be called to the front, where they could blow out the candles. The teacher pointed to the ornate filigree ceiling rose above us, which she said was where fairies lived. One of them had provided a penny as a present. *Where was mine? This wasn't fair, why should this girl have a penny and not me?* So I screamed the place down. I was sent to the headmistress. The door to her office had a tiny metal knocker in the shape of a lady wearing a crinoline and bonnet. I was asked to sit on the chair and I noticed an ornament on her desk: an old-fashioned carriage with two little people inside. The Head noticed me looking at it.

'Why are you here?'

'I wanted a penny.'

'And who sent you to see me?'

'Miss Trotter sent me.'

She nodded towards the carriage.

'You can play with it, if you wish.'

I spent a very pleasant five minutes rolling the carriage back and forth across her desk.

'You can go back to your classroom now,' she said kindly.

When Mam came to collect me, my coat was missing so she played holy war with the teacher. It was discovered to be in the house area. I must have taken it off after outdoor play and forgot – I was set to inherit Mam's poor memory.

For the first couple of months I tagged along with any mother going in the direction of the school. It was on the lane at the top of my street so the journey was very safe. As I became more confident, it wasn't necessary to stick so close to my adopted parent, so one day as I sauntered along, eating an apple, the older sister of a lass in my class snatched it from my hand and grabbed me by the back of the neck as she scrubbed it into my face. With nobody there to protect me, this was an extremely scary experience. I didn't see it coming and I don't know why she did it. Mam's friend Irene had a daughter, Lynne, in the same class as this girl and when she found out, she grabbed her after school and bashed her all over the lane. I was never bothered by her again.

Usually, arguments were quite innocent slanging matches, such as, 'My dad's bigger than your dad', but sometimes they grew more serious and we became involved in 'Pelting Stones' – a very exciting game until you were hit by one. Another danger was if you strayed into new territory and fresh dangers presented themselves, like the day me and a pal walked along a lane in Scotswood. A lad ran out from his backyard and threatened us with violence unless we sat on the path. This we did, but then he brought some broken glass and commanded us to sit on it. We were scared of him as he made a lot of noise, but on further reflection, there were two of us and he was smaller, so I stood up and said as loud as I could, 'No, we won't!'

The slightest flicker of defeat crossed his face before he asserted himself once more, but I had seen that giveaway sign, which street kids are well aware of. We walked off and he scuttled back in his lair without a roar.

Our school was an old Victorian building with what seemed like lots of stone staircases leading all over the place. The ceilings were high and the toilets were across the yard outside, next to a disused air-raid shelter. I can recall going into the boiler room with a friend's mother. Her husband was the boiler man and he was shovelling coal into it. I still remember being fascinated by the brilliant white light from the fire and the dry heat smell of coke burning.

The first half term meant time off school and I was off to my grandparents' in Gateshead. When I returned home at the weekend, I just hung around the house, but come Monday, I went to the shops with Mam. She always met half a dozen women on the way there and back and stopped to chat while I rolled around the pavement in pure boredom, hopping, stamping, anything to break the monotony, when one neighbour asked:

'Why is she off school, doesn't look like there's anything wrong with her?'

'She's not off sick, the school is on holiday.'

'No, they went back today.'

'Ah well, she can go in tomorrow.'

No panic at all, but of course she couldn't admit to the

teacher that she had simply forgotten, so it became necessary to write a note.

'Ken, how do you spell diarrhoea?'

'D... i... a...'

'D... i...'

'a... r...'

'Hang on a minute, D... i...'

'a... r, man!'

'D... i... a... a...'

'No, D... i... a... r...'

'Oh, forget it! I'll just put upset stomach.'

* * *

The form teacher called the register every morning:

'Jane Smith?'

'Present, Miss Trotter.'

'Anne Robson?'

'Present, Miss Trotter.'

After registration children brought their little tin to her desk with the correct change of dinner money. It was quite a cruel practice of teachers to mention the names of those who were taking free dinners. Children with a father out of work or from a single-parent family were immediately singled out. One lad from a large family was the owner of a knitted swimming costume, an old matted jumper which his mother had cut the sleeves off and sewed a crotch into. He did not escape the sleeves either as they were sealed at each end and he had to wear them as socks, big bulky things in his shoes.

It must have been so uncomfortable, but families didn't waste anything back then.

Mothers also bought jumpers from jumble sales to pull the wool out with the intention of creating new ones. Children in the family would be employed to unravel, wash and dry the wool, then stand with their arms out while it was wound around them. A man's jumper from a sale would be prized as it would provide two children's garments.

Children were often given jobs to do for the teachers. I was asked to take the cups of tea to the staff, so I negotiated my way with a cup and saucer with a biscuit on the side down around six sets of worn stone steps and into the yard, where Mr Scott was on yard duty. He said, 'Oh, I don't eat biscuits, you can have it.'

It was the loveliest taste, a custard cream. He swigged his tea quickly and gave me back the cup and saucer. On my return to collect another cuppa, the secretary said, 'And this one is for Mr Scott.'

'But I've just given him his tea.'

'Mr Scott doesn't like biscuits.'

She looked at the saucer, then at me.

I swiped my hand across my mouth.

'This time, get it right! Take this to Mrs Clarke.'

I didn't get the job again.

Mr Scott was new to the school – a very good-looking man, something that was also appreciated by Miss Belling. Being a woman who always wore her hair in a bun, she suddenly began to adopt a Diana Dors style, peering through one side of her hair while the other side was wrapped around her ear. Mr Scott took our class as form teacher and one of the first lessons showed our lack of knowledge. A map of the world was hung over the blackboard and he proceeded to point to various countries. We didn't recognise any of them, even Britain was unknown to us.

'What have these people been teaching you?'

Of course, being from our area, we were on the scrapheap before we even got going. What was the point, was their philosophy? We were all headed for factory work anyway in their minds. Mr Scott set to by changing the lines of desks into sets, pushing the desks together in groups, and children were organised by ability. Every Friday, he put the wireless on and you could hear a pin drop: this time it was a talk on Darwin and evolution.

Miss Belling was more interested in how things looked so we had to decorate the margins of our poetry books with flowers and birds and suchlike. We were given inkwells, italic pens and shown how to write in italics.

'Hold your pens at forty-five degrees!'

During a swapping session with friends I was given two Penny Red stamps, so I took them into school to show the teacher. I forgot to take them with me at playtime and when I returned, someone had stuffed them in my inkwell.

When a supply teacher was assigned to our class we were asked to draw a house. It was common practice for us kids to draw the house square in the middle of the page with a little winding path with a garden, although none of us possessed one. The rooms could be seen and the light bulbs in each room aglow with light denoted by little lines forking outwards. No shades, what were they? A bed and kitchen with chairs drawn sideways on so they looked as if there were only two legs. I was first finished so I took my drawing to the teacher's desk to be marked.

'What's this? Can you see into someone's living room from the street? No! Go away and draw me walls, houses have walls.'

As I returned to my seat, everyone else was scribbling away furiously. This is what I call a 'creative injury' – I loved drawing and this experience didn't deter me in later years, but what of those children who were affected by her lack of imagination? Thankfully, things have changed.

One teacher used to assign a couple of lads to wash his car on Friday afternoons. It was his pride and joy until after lessons one day when he returned to find the wheels gone, it was propped up on bricks and most of the accessories, such as wing mirrors and badges, had also disappeared.

Helen was a lass in my class who I sat next to for a while. She brought *The Bobbsey Twins* annuals into school and all of us girls wanted to read them. Her family went to Amsterdam for holidays and she was forever blatting on about tulips – there were tulip paintings in her home and various flower-related ornaments. I loved *The Little Match Girl*, *The Tinder Box* and *The Little Tin Soldier* stories. She was good fun and a right giggler. After being kept behind at the end of one school day for misbehaving, Helen and I were leaving by the main door when a man approached us.

'Do you recognise this woman?'

'No.'

We didn't particularly take much notice of the faces as the group of adult males and females were naked, posing for a photo, all lined up as if they were at a wedding, brazen-faced.

'This is Miss R,' he said, 'she goes to a nudist colony.'

What was that? But we didn't wait to find out and ran to Helen's flat, which was just behind the school. Her mother was peeling potatoes in a dish at the sink when we told her. Without putting the knife down, she pelted down the stone back stairs into the lane, shouting, 'Where *is* he, where the bloody hell is he?'

She ran into the corner shop brandishing the knife at any men in there who were innocently buying cigarettes. We were close at her heels and managed to say that he wasn't among them. The police were called to the school next day and me and Helen were interviewed separately. Nothing more was mentioned and we didn't find out if they caught the man. It was probably a vindictive ex-boyfriend, that's if it really was Miss R in the photo. Who could say?

Random men were not the only criminals connected with the school. One day, every class attended assembly to be faced with a wall of hymn books, prayer books and Bibles on the hall floor. There were dozens and dozens of them. Two girls were paraded in front of them and Miss Belling marched back and forth while the girls looked down, shamefaced, at the parquet flooring.

'These two girls have been systematically stealing books from the school.'

Where on earth they were storing them in the small flats we all lived in is anyone's guess, but even more puzzling was why they wanted them in the first place.

The assembly hall was also used for singing practice. Our class was chosen to represent the school in a contest to be held at the Newcastle City Hall. The chosen song was 'Wintry Winds'. On the day of the competition we were taken to the venue by Miss Belling. When we removed our coats, she was aghast at my outfit: Mam had shoved me out the door that morning after putting this yellow sundress and matching bolero out for me to wear. It had a washed-out ink stain right on the front. Miss Belling took me by the top of my arm and roughly marched me out into the hallway.

'We are representing our school and you turn up like this! You are a mess, a *mess*, do you hear? There are very prestigious schools here – Dame Allan, Jesmond – from all over the city. You will not stand in the front, I want you right at the back of the choir!'

She ensured that this was carried out personally. I was the shortest in my class and couldn't see a thing, but I sang my heart out anyway.

* * *

The cloakrooms were a place of fun, huge wooden walls with arched metal bars which joined each one together. I was swinging back and forth when Ann decided that it would be a good idea to practise a flying trapeze move. She hung onto my ankles and set herself swinging, but I couldn't hold on and went smack onto the concrete floor. My back was numb and I couldn't move. Mr Scott was called and accompanied me to hospital until Mam arrived from work. I was off school for six weeks, severely bruised – I spent the time with the Romes at Gateshead as Mam couldn't take time off.

I missed valuable lessons in arithmetic, although having said that, I wasn't any good at it anyway. The only table I learned by rote was the 'eights', and that was as a punishment for something I had done in class. Even now, if anyone asks me what five times eight is I have to go through the rhyme to tell them. I also shudder at the mention of 'If it takes six men two hours to dig a hole, how long will it take one man?'

I was well into writing poetry and always on the lookout for a subject. Around this time, the Bay of Pigs crisis was being played out in Cuba between America and the Soviet Union and I was really worried that trouble was going to find its way to our shores. I wrote a poem after a vivid dream which involved three tanks going up one of the streets in Benwell. An earth was on top of each tank: the first was green with water, the second engulfed in red and orange flames and the third was black. Two people were in the dream: one stood watching from the side of the road and the other was in front, sitting on a wooden bench. The Vickers factory was in the distance. The only line I recall was '*The skies were grey and bled*'. Later, my brother David painted a picture of this dream after I explained it to him.

During a poetry session held by Miss Belling, she called me out to the front of the class, threw my poem onto her desk and said accusingly, 'You didn't write this, you copied from somewhere!'

She wouldn't listen to me when I insisted it was mine and sent me back to my seat.

A few weeks later, I was to have my revenge. Mam had been given a matted, shrunken jumper from a neighbour.

'It will do for your Yvonne.'

It was a cream lumpy thing with a V-neck far too low for me so I pinned a glass brooch to close the gap. I wore it for assembly in the upper hall one morning and noticed that as Miss Belling charged back and forth at the front, she blinked as something irritated her eye. Quickly, I realised my brooch was casting a glint from the sunshine blasting through the window, so each time she was facing forward, I positioned that brooch with a flick of a finger and throughout assembly, and much to my delight the old bugger was tortured. I dread to think what would have happened had she discovered my wickedness.

The upper hall was also used for dancing and games on rainy days. Music was put on via an old record player and we pranced around happily until a bully of a lad in our class took great delight in pushing into the girls to knock them over. The teacher made him sit on the pipe running around the circumference of the hall. He began to fidget out of boredom and as he bounced up and down, his head dislodged the fire extinguisher, which crashed to the floor and set off a stream of water and foam. The bottle began to spin and shot off across the room, kids were screaming, yelling and dashing in all directions, while the teacher tried to regain control. A brave little lad who hadn't been in our class long as he had been living in Australia – Jimmy was his name – threw himself onto the bottle and slowed it down.

The hall walls were decorated with an enormous frieze with a Greek mythology theme which our class had taken great pride in recreating over the period of a couple of months: full-sized Theseus and the Minotaur, The Labyrinth and Jason and the Golden Fleece. We had worked tirelessly to build up the stories in pictures. However, there was a fight in the classroom one day during crafts and a particularly naughty lad called Rob stuck a pair of scissors into the arm of a lad called Trevor and began to range around the room, holding the weapon above his head. Everyone screamed and Mr Scott pinned him down over a desk. Books and desks were strewn about as Rob kicked and struck out at the teacher. He eventually broke free and ran from the classroom into the hall. We all followed in total disbelief but that emotion turned to pure rage as we witnessed the little sod dragging his hand through the centre of our frieze all the way down the hall. Poor Trevor was nursing his arm while all this was going on.

* * *

When the Eleven Plus test was given out I did well in subjects such as English, Art and History, but for Arithmetic, I was informed that I had secured just one mark, which was only given for my name at the top of the page. Really, I had tried. Mr Scott was pulling out all the plugs to help us and for the first time gave out homework. When I read, 'If it takes ten men five hours to dig a hole, how long will it take one man?', I was in a right panic. I can remember feeling utter despair as I pleaded with my parents for advice on multiplication and long division to no avail. Next, from one to the other in the Rome household, which only resulted in a mass argument on who knew best, but none of them did. Back home on the Sunday night, Sarah had a dozen pals round to hers. I asked everyone and only one lad stepped forward. Give him his due, he battled for a good hour but I still couldn't get long division hence I was destined for a telling-off – and for Atkinson Road Secondary Modern at the top of the hill.

At 'Akky Road', as it was known locally, the classes were made up of our lot from South Benwell, together with kids from other schools, all of whom hadn't 'passed'. I remember feeling really put out at having 'failed' as it was put to us. We secretly envied the schoolmates who had secured places at Rutherford, Pendower and John Marlay schools.

But I was soon to forget the 'shame' of being second best on meeting the other kids in my new class. Kenneth Fairbanks was cool, he had a quiff kept in place with Brylcreem. He got the nickname 'Fairy', but it didn't bother him – he was too laid-back for that. I took a temporary dislike to him when he laughed at my bathing suit at our weekly lesson. Mam had bought me this horrible lilac thing, with rows and rows of flounce. I looked like a dirigible balloon and it earned me the nickname of 'Frilly Bathers' for a while until, thankfully, I was given a new one.

Older pupils were on the verge of leaving school to secure jobs. The lasses tatted their hair into Beehives, hair lacquer was sprayed liberally, but anyone who couldn't afford it used a sugar-and-water solution. This attracted the bees, so maybe that's where the name 'Beehive' comes from. The Beatles had just become popular and one of the older lasses had a white Sloppy Joe jumper on with 'The BEETLES' written on the back in pen and an 'A' written over the top of the second 'E'. I had a little guitar badge with John Lennon inside a plastic picture circle.

I had begun standing in the corner of the yard with some of the older lasses. They smoked and seemed very risqué to me. One of them offered me 'a drag' of her cigarette and gave me instructions to suck in as hard as I could. Much to her delight, this burned my throat, but she probably did me a favour, as I was never tempted to try again. Besides, some of them picked up used fags and pulled out any remaining strands of tobacco to make a roll-your-own, which I found disgusting. My precious badge was nicked that day in the schoolyard and it wouldn't have surprised me if it was that lass who took it. I have since seen the whole Fab Four set displayed in York Museum – I loved that badge.

The girls in my class took cookery lessons, which were split into weeks of either cooking, cleaning the ovens and pans or hygiene instruction. I once cooked a dish which involved an onion. I'd left it on the boil too long and it burned, leaving a black stain on the pan. I couldn't be bothered to clean it so pushed it back onto the shelf. During afternoon break, Sarah also had a cookery session in her class and it was her turn on cleaning duty.

'Some bugger put a manky pan back on the shelf and it took all afternoon to get the black off it!' she moaned.

I didn't own up.

For one hygiene lesson, we were asked to bring in a hairbrush. Each girl placed a piece of newspaper on her knee. A lass called Lynn Jones always came to school with the greasiest hair, her mop was known as 'rat's tails'. After brushing, everyone commented how lustrous her shiny hair was, we couldn't get over it. But it was never like that again.

Mam was in her element that I was taking cookery at school. Once every three weeks, she didn't have to think about placing a tin of beans or a packet of cheese on the table and could leave it to me to create Cornish pasties or corned beef pie. The teacher announced that we were all to make Fish Surprise and to bring in a tin of salmon for the next lesson.

'What does she think she's on,' said Mam, 'her granny's yacht?'

'Mam, I've got to have it, Teacher said! Everyone else will have a tin of salmon. *Please*, Mam?'

I went on and on until she relented. The dish consisted of mashed potato and salmon with breadcrumbs on the top. The teacher was annoyed because when she said 'breadcrumbs', we thought she meant to bring in a slice of bread, so she was forced to use all of her box of breadcrumbs on our fish pies. I took it home and put it on the table. Mam stuck her fork into it and tasted some.

'Why, it's nothing but a giant fish cake! What a waste of a tin of salmon!'

I didn't mention that all the other girls had used pilchards or sardines – they mustn't have whinged so much at their mothers.

I discovered Eggy Bread, a slice of bread dipped into raw whipped-up egg and fried, so at least this was something I could do myself. It was hardly a culinary masterpiece but a change from cheese and tomatoes. Besides, cheese was becoming a bore. Dad consumed copious amounts of the stuff and even if it had mould on it, he simply sliced the green parts off. Mam said that if it was off on the outside, it was certainly off on the inside, but this still didn't deter him or encourage her to vary the range so unless I learned of a new recipe at school, flavourless fare was à la carte in our house.

* * *

I loved History lessons with Miss Jones. She taught us about the Seven Wonders of the World and I was entranced by the Ziggurat at Ur. Mr Bell sometimes taught us singing and was an excellent pianist, which inspired us to sing louder. He would crash his fingers on the keys, whizzing up and down the scales. But our regular teacher for Music was a very hefty lady who favoured singing the same songs at every lesson – 'Camptown Races', 'The Water of Tyne' and 'Cushie Butterfield' among her repertoire. She had to leave the room one day and in her absence, one of the lads put a drawing pin on her chair. When she came back in, we were all terrified she would get hurt, but didn't dare say anything for fear of this lad. One brave soul, Graham, spoke up before she put her weight on the pin. She just assumed it had dropped there, so a huge sigh of relief went up.

Mr Kane was a Maths teacher. He caught a lad reading a comic during his lesson, clipped him around the ear with it and said, 'Boy, if you are going to read a comic in my class, please have the sense to hide it behind a book!'

Of course, this gave carte blanche to the rest of us for future reference. Jerry wasn't a confident lad and Mr Kane knew this so always asked him to read to the class. He started off quite slowly and then began rabbiting so fast to get it over with. None of us were laughing: Jerry was one of our own.

John Coleman's family owned a shop which sold fresh fish, he was also a shy lad and a little slow. He came to school one day with his pyjamas clearly visible under his clothing, the hems covered his shoes below the trousers and the collar peeped over his shirt. Kane took it upon himself to bring John to the front of the class, ribbing him about his attire.

'Is it chilly today, Coleman? Did you find it necessary to insulate yourself today? As a punishment, you will bring me some fishcakes tomorrow.'

He looked around the room, waiting for a laugh and approval of his behaviour, but he received none.

I was surprised that I didn't become the butt of his jokes as I was so poor at Arithmetic and he was supposed to be teaching that very subject. With hindsight, I don't suppose he even looked at our work to mark it. Yes, this reinforced the notion that we were classed as fodder for the factory.

English classes were well-liked, with Mr Cooper at the helm. He looked and sounded like the comedian Frankie Howerd. He was nicknamed 'Mad Jack' because he didn't take any nonsense from the older kids at the school, who were noted for causing some teachers to burst into tears, pelting chalk, blackboard rubbers at each other, running around in class and clashing the lids of their desks. One day, MJ announced that he was going to write his new song on the board. He proceeded to chalk the lyrics to 'Swinging On A Star', to which everyone began shouting out and laughing.

'Sir, somebody already wrote that!'

'Diiiid theyyyyyy nowww?'

We became really excited and jolly, then he snapped and began throwing chalk at us. We were ordered to read to ourselves. *Jock of the Bushveld* was the group book and a lass called Kathleen was so engrossed, she shouted out, 'Mam, put the kettle on!'

Everyone fell about laughing. Kathleen was ordered to stand in the corner for the rest of the lesson.

Still, he wasn't as bad as one teacher at the neighbouring Denton School, who used a water pistol to fire at pupils!

* * *

Science lessons were offered by Mrs Clements. She demonstrated the dangers of smoking by puffing through a white handkerchief, which turned the fabric yellowy blue.

'This is what's deposited on your lungs, it's tar.'

She organised a trip to the local General Hospital, where we were treated to observing a set of lungs floating in jars of formaldehyde for research purposes. The doctor pointed out the white patches on the organs. He explained that when a person has a smoker's cough, it is due to the lungs hardening and turning the texture like that of a leather shoe. They find it difficult to breathe, he said, and this causes cancer. I often wonder if any of the smokers in our class who sneaked out to the toilets across the yard continued to do so after that day.

The main hall was used for morning assembly, as a dining area and for gym lessons and country dancing. There were wooden climbing bars from floor to ceiling on the walls. I was sent on an errand one day. As I walked around the balcony there was a sports lesson going on, with older lads jumping over the horse and climbing up ropes. One lad hated these lessons so persuaded his mates to hide him inside the box, where he sat until it was finished, listening to the thudding as lads vaulted over him. The school took delivery of new Velcro-edged rubber mats with sponge inside. This lad decided that he would take part for a change and wrapped a mat around himself. With only head and feet on show, he shuffled round the polished oak floor, shouting, 'I am a Dalek!' The headmaster glared from his office and then raged over the balcony, 'You, boy! You stupid boy, get up here NOW!'

The lad got such a shock that he went over like a felled tree, trapped on the floor like a giant sausage roll, until someone tore the Velcro apart. Such a daftie but at least he was allowed

Woodwork lessons, which the girls were barred from. I wanted to make a coffee table or an ashtray like the boys did (not that we'd have used an ashtray for its intended purpose in our house as my parents didn't smoke), so why was this not allowed? For all I enjoyed sewing and cookery lessons I could never understand this. Surely there were some lads who didn't enjoy practical skills and they could have allowed the odd lass into the Woodwork room, but we were never given the option (it wasn't until the nineties that I began a course where I learned carving, how to use a lathe and a bandsaw). Mam bought me a sewing machine – a Jones electric with a pedal, it was iron and weighed a ton. All of the ones I had seen before this were old treadle models. I chose it at the Co-op on Newgate Street and couldn't wait for it to be delivered so I begged her to allow me to bring it home there and then. I dragged it along the path, this iron giant, stopping every few minutes, but she refused to help. Of course, one of the first things she did once I mastered its use was to go to Farnon's department store to buy fabric and curtain tape!

Mam wasn't big on ironing (or washing, come to that). I made a gorgeous cream corduroy skirt and first time in the wash, she hung it dripping wet on a rusty rail in the cupboard – the red stain went right through it. I took care of my own laundry after that. But with both my parents, I had a problem with anything new which I purchased. Dad worked in a garage and had a stupid habit of washing his oily hands in the sink. Before rinsing them, he would pick any item from the basket and 'Get the thick off'. More things were ruined in this way.

CHAPTER THREE

Catechism, Camping and the China Cabinet

St Aidan's was an old Protestant Gothic church and hall which stood on the corner of St John's Road and Joseph Street in Elswick. As children, we knew that if we stood outside long enough on Saturdays, there was bound to be a wedding. As the happy couple drove away, it was customary to throw coins out onto the street (known locally as 'The Hoy Oot'). There would be a mad scramble and we picked up as much as we could get our hands on.

Waiting for the couple to become man and wife, I noticed a lad who had caught a starling. He told me that he was training it – he was a falconer and it would come back to him like the eagles do. He had tied the poor creature's legs with string and began whirling it around so the legs were pulled from their sockets – I couldn't bear to see this.

However, we all knew that if anyone had tried to stop him, we'd have been beaten up.

This wasn't the first time I had witnessed such barbarity. Me and Sarah used to go over St John's graveyard after church to look for a lonely-looking plot on which we could put a few daisies or clover to 'decorate it'. One day, an older lad was intentionally pulling the legs from a homing pigeon to take the little metal identification rings.

Some of the kids in the area were little criminals in the making. I once saw a group of wasters stealing bottles of Domestos from a shop. They emptied the contents onto the grass, then went back in to claim the pennies back from returns. But none of this was so disturbing as what some did to defenceless wild creatures.

* * *

Christmas bazaars and jumble sales were held at St Aidan's, but never garden fêtes, as the back of the church grounds were covered in weeds. One year, Mam saved up in the church club to buy a dinner service – although she didn't attend services, she liked the fairs. The cups were painted inside and out (and the plates and saucers too) with a hunting scene, dogs and horses with riders in red coats. 'It's real bone china!' she kept saying. She aspired to own a china cabinet one day, so this set would definitely not be in use.

There was always a good supply of volunteers to man stalls. I enjoyed listening to the women chattering and discussing what the other members of the congregation were wearing, including the Vicar's wife. Half the time I didn't understand what they meant, some of it went over my head, but I craned my neck to hear.

'She's always beautifully dressed, that shows respect.'

'Yes, I love that frock she wore today and she always bows so low before Communion that her knee touches the floor.'

'Very respectful, very respectful.'

'But he's trying to make it too High Church.'

I do remember that the Reverend gathered a few of us together to introduce Confession.

'What's that?' we asked.

'We all need to be sorry for our sins,' he said.

But this wasn't to be done in boxed-off cubbies, as in Catholic churches, but in the pews next to each other. We sat there trying to think of something we had done wrong, so he helped us along a little.

'Maybe you have been unkind to a friend?'

Yes, that would do, so we all offered that up as our Confession. The idea didn't catch on.

His next project was for us to be shepherded into Confirmation. Around six of us showed an interest, me and my pal Sarah, who knew about such things.

'It means you get bread and wine on Sundays.'

This sounded OK to me so we signed up. So we met at the Church House, family home of the Reverend and his wife and two children. We were led through the vestibule into a library – a library in someone's home? The most luxurious space I had ever experienced, there were beautifully bound leather volumes, a writing desk and paintings on the walls. It sure beat the socks off Dad's Charles Atlas body building manual. When I asked Mam why he used it, she said, 'Because he doesn't want anyone to kick sand in his face.'

She read me a story when a book was sent home from school by a teacher. It was about a little pink pig and I have always held that memory. I felt so secure, cuddled up to her. It never happened again. Around then I was also becoming increasingly aware of arguments between my parents which ceased when I walked into the room.

Anyway, floor-to-ceiling bookcases lined the four walls of the vicarage, there was a huge desk, patterned carpets and a coal fire surrounded by beautiful patterned tiles and a golden fender with a little stand nearby, sporting a brush and shovel. This seemed like a mansion to me, coming from a damp, near-crumbling property as I did. There was a bay window in our front bedroom which leaked water when it rained, so buckets were plentiful in our gaff. Our homes were labelled unfit for human habitation before World War II. They had been solid structures, but weren't kept in good enough repair.

In the end there were only two of us going to read and learn the Catechism and then Sarah dropped out after a few more sessions because she couldn't memorise any of the text. But I loved sitting in that room so it was worth it. When the Reverend asked me who I would like my sponsor to be, he could tell from my blank expression that I hadn't a clue what that meant, so he volunteered, saying:

'I do know a very nice parishioner who would be willing to take on the role. She will guide you in the church, a little like a godparent.'

Mrs Anderson presented me with a prayer book covered in plum leather, which I still have to this day. Also, a tiny little box. I opened it and inside was the most beautiful real silver cross and chain. Wow! It was delicately patterned in a kind of Celtic design. That was the last contact I had with her.

I did join the Brownies. One of the older members of the group gave me a brown dress of dull brushed cotton and I was given a spare hat and yellow tie from the Brown Owl. Tawny Owl was in charge of putting us into our groups: there were Elves, Gnomes and I was placed with the Pixies.

This is what we do the Elves, think of others not ourselves.

Here you see the laughing Gnomes, helping Mother in our homes.

Look out, we're the jolly Pixies, helping people when in fixes.

Fair enough, not too many words to learn, but it came to the time when parents were invited to watch us perform a little play on the stage in the hall. Brown Owl decided as there weren't enough groups, she created another one called Sprites and took one girl from each of the existing groups. This happened on the night of the show.

Here we come, the sprightly Sprites, brave and helpful like the knights.

But it wound up a complete mix of the songs we had already learned in our respective groups and descended into a jumble of incoherence. My parents didn't attend, which was probably just as well.

We were told there were many badges of achievement and our first task was to use a public phone box to make a call. Tawny Owl would be near the phone in the vestry and we were to find the nearest street where one could be found. She gave us some pennies and off we went. It seemed to take ages to find a phone box that hadn't been vandalised. Being short arses, it took all three of us to pull the heavy iron door open and we could hardly see what we were doing in there. We made so many mistakes that we lost the money. Probably because we didn't understand that button B had to be pressed to retrieve it! I'm sure both Tawny and Brown Owl thought we had purloined the cash.

Every now and then there would be a games evening at the church: Hangman and Beetle Drives. On Sundays, after service and the coffee morning, the men played billiards or snooker. I never knew which, only that they used a green table, knocked balls around with cues and wrote numbers on a board with chalk. It was really addictive to watch.

As I was about to celebrate my Confirmation Day in church, the Reverend dropped into our house on his rounds in the neighbourhood. There was a tin of sardines on the table. Mam pretended they had been left out by mistake.

'Oh, what's that doing there?' she said, picking it up swiftly and putting it back in the kitchen cabinet.

'We don't eat those very often,' she added.

Oh yes, we bloody do! I thought, but didn't say anything.

I have no memory of Mam's attendance at my Confirmation, but I do know that Dad was definitely not there as he was always out doing his own thing.

I was asked by another girl in my class to attend a social evening at her place of worship, which was on Buddle Road, a Methodist church. Tea was served in cups with saucers. Mine was too hot so I poured a little into the saucer and blew on it to cool it down. I was never asked again, but kept badgering her.

'My mam says you can't come back,' was the eventual explanation.

Maybe I was slurping. For a while I felt common, but it was really Mam's fault for not using the bone china.

* * *

I joined St Aidan's Guiding community when I was a little older. Once more, I was given a hand-me-down: this time a navy wool skirt from a friend's elder sister, who had grown out of it. I went to the house to pick it up. The family had a little Westie dog, which was old and blind and kept bumping into furniture – he only moved out of the basket to go for a pee. The skirt was so lovely, I even wore it for everyday use. We did similar activities to the Brownies, but the badges were gained from more complicated tasks: cookery, for one. I couldn't very well ask advice from my mam as she didn't cook.

She set out a dinner once a week on Sundays: lumpy gravy, lumpy potatoes and tinned meat. On occasion she would attempt a roast. We had a set of six Pyrex dishes with lids (there was only one left without a lid by the time we moved house). Once the meat had been placed on a plate, she had a habit of dunking the dish in cold water straight from the oven so it cracked clean in half. Otherwise she would plonk a bag of tomatoes and a half pound of cheese on the table, or a tin of beans or sardines. After lunch, she dismantled the pipes of the oven, cleaned and put them back together and it wasn't in use again until the following Sunday. But she did make a very lovely rice pudding on Sundays: egg, milk, rice and lots of sugar, always with a skin on top. It sat in a metal dish on a low heat for a couple of hours.

Nivea cream was Mam's favourite: she dotted three dollops on her forehead, one on her nose, chin and each cheek. It was massaged into her face like she was making pastry, only she never did that. She used block mascara, which was sold with a little brush – she spat on the brush and scraped it across the black block, then applied it to her lashes. A disgusting practice! Next, she began plucking her eyebrows and I was roped in for this task. She always seemed to ask me to do this when I was on my way out. I wasn't paying attention during one session and nipped a chunk of skin instead of a hair – she didn't ask me again after that.

After going to see a film starring Elizabeth Taylor, Mam

purchased a black stick with which to give the impression that she had a beauty spot.

'Mam, you've got a black mark just above your lip!'

'It's a beauty spot. Liz Taylor has one and she's the most beautiful woman in the world.'

She was easily distracted and pair this with a poor memory and the results won't be favourable. Mam went through her usual beauty routine of dabbing Nivea, then rushed out to the Co-op. Later in the day, when I called in, the staff were having a right giggle behind the counter and each time I put in my request to be served, they became more hysterical.

'What are you laughing at?'

'Your mam was in the shop earlier.'

'And?'

'She hadn't rubbed her cream in.'

More guffawing.

I could just imagine her standing there like Coco the Clown while they all suppressed their laughter. Local tradespeople, if they shared notes, could have made a comedy series. When the window cleaner was chasing Mam up the street on her way to work one day, she just kept on running and shouted, 'I will pay you tonight, I'm in a hurry!'

He kept on chasing, and when he caught up with her, it was to remove a dry-cleaning ticket from the back of her coat.

As soon as the sun came out, Mam would park her backside in a deckchair in the backyard. Of course, as the sun didn't come out that often in the North of England, she forgot from one year to the next how to put it up. One day, I watched from the sitting room window as she pulled it about like a cat's cradle game.

'Ken, come and put this bloody thing up, will you?'

When the sun went around to the front of the house, Mam never wasted any time and simply upped sticks and sat in the front street. She was the only person among the rows of terraced flats to do this – all the other wives were cooking, cleaning or ironing – and she'd be there until the last sign of sun. There might be a momentary lapse if our massive Manx cat Lucy was fighting a dog in the lane. Lucy ran the walls of the backyards hissing at other moggies and occasionally jumping from a great height onto the back of any passing dog.

'Get in here, you stupid thing!' Mam would say. Then it was back to the important business of sun soaking. When she eventually came back indoors, she was greeted by the arrangements on the kitchen table. Dad liked to line up the condiment set, cutlery, cups, anything that happened to be there. Mam would get really ratty, 'Look at him, he's got everything arranged like a regiment of soldiers!'

Then she would scrabble everything up. He knew when she was in a fuming temper that it was better to say nothing.

* * *

So, I was on my own for that badge. But the next thing on the agenda was a week's trip to Felton, a little village about an hour's travelling from Newcastle. A farmer had agreed to allow us Guides on his land with our tents and latrines. We were told there would be the odd cow roaming around, but they wouldn't harm us. Those of us whose families were not in possession of a car hitched a ride with others more affluent. We were to bring a few changes of clothing, a tin plate and mug. We lasses were split into groups to put our tents up. There was a competition for the first finished, but we came last and were still on with it until it was becoming dark. People who had long since set theirs up, erected the latrines and food tents came to help. The ground sheets slipped out from under the tent and I was terrified of the insects.

It was just as well that I came from a home where adventures in food preparation were never a priority. I will never forget the taste of battered spam cooked swimming in fat. A girl called Carol was in charge of making the jelly for afters: she was wearing a purple jumper at the time and everyone was picking bits of mohair from the jelly.

A visit to the toilet during the night was a hazardous affair. On one side there were sloping banks, which led down to a fast-flowing stream; on the other, cowpats to negotiate. Once the deed was done, you were responsible for digging a hole to cover your tracks.

It was a miserable time, but there were some highlights when we held concerts in the big tent: some singing, joke telling and comedy routines. Someone sang 'Everyone's Gone To The Moon', another reminder of our misery. One younger girl cried for her mother for the first couple of days and was told that she would perk up soon. Until it REALLY began to rain and we were flooded out of our tents.

The farmer housed us in a barn which had been used to

store grain. There were huge orange chutes from the roof, which we had to wend our way past, and straw on the floor. Lasses were continually bumping their heads. I was afraid of the insects in the tent, but this was something else – there were what seemed like hundreds of spiders. This sent the tearful girl over the edge and her parents were called to take her home. How I wished that I had had the foresight to cadge a lift, but this only occurred to me after she left.

On Sunday, we walked a mile or so into the village to attend the local church service. All of my socks had been ruined by cow shit so I had to borrow a pair from one of the older girls. They were so big, they flopped over my shoes – you might say I had that 'rural look' as I resembled a Shire horse. Four of us lagged behind on the way back to camp and a group of village lads on bicycles terrorised us, riding their bikes around us and blocking our way. Then at last it was time to return home, me with a puffy eye from a chute bump and socks beyond washing clean.

Mam wasn't about so I invited my friends into my parents' bedroom to show off her selection of new clothes: a red satin dress with a black bodice, pink flowered shift and a pale blue suit.

'Ooh, that's lovely!'

'She wears this one when she goes to the Cavendish nightclub.'

Mam was meeting new friends who went to Grey's Club, Billy Botto's and the Picadilly – mostly casino cocktail affairs with cabaret singers. She and Dad hardly spoke to each other through the week. He went to the Westfield Social Club at one end of the road and if she was playing out nearer home, she attended the Milvain Social Club at the other end. It wasn't until I was in my teens that I really began to realise how dysfunctional my parents' marriage was.

Mam finally managed to save enough money to buy her coveted china cabinet. It had patterned silver glass on the front and sides held together with ivory melamine. The shelves were of clear glass and she wasted no time in polishing and placing her dinner service and other bits and bobs inside. A little irony there that she polished and cleaned the dining table and cabinet and china within an inch of their lives, but had no time to cook or lay the table.

* * *

As I opened the front door at Buddle Road one day, three children stood on the top step. I was eleven years of age and had no knowledge of their existence.

'I'm Kath and this is my sister Lil and brother Billy, we are your cousins.'

Their mother Beattie was Dad's sister. Now that explained everything: Mam's family was known to me, but Dad didn't keep in touch with any of his. I was made up to know these great kids. They were impressed that I had my own bedroom. The china cabinet must have made an impression too as it stood imposingly full of expensive china which took a year to save up for.

Being an only child, I was always told how lucky I was to

have all of my toys to myself and how I didn't have to trail younger siblings round with me, but all I really wanted was someone to trail around. One of my friends – Sarah – had a younger sister, who was the canniest little bairn.

'I've got to bring our Pauline with me!' she complained. But I would have loved her as a little sister.

For me this was a godsend – for the first time I was presented with relatives who weren't adults.

'While we're here,' said Kath, 'we're going to visit Mrs Mooney [an old friend of our Mam's]. Do you want to come?'

Did I want to come? Of course!

So, off we went along Buddle Road and down to the bottom of Maria Street.

'I was born there at number 17,' I said, pointing across the street.

'Yes, we know, our mam lived at number 22,' Kath informed me.

Beattie had talked about us and her old neighbours – I had so much to catch up on.

Kath took charge once more and knocked on the door. A voice from the other side announced that she was on her way and to wait. After the initial introduction, Mrs Mooney invited us into her upstairs flat, walking badly, hauling herself up by way of the banister. She slumped in her chair in front of the fireplace. I was fascinated by a set of false teeth floating in water, they looked huge through the thick glass. Mrs M scooped them up and stuck them in her mouth – they looked considerably smaller out of the solution. Lil was practising her reading skills on the various medications lined up along the top of the fireplace.

'Al… ka… sel… selsa, Philo… san.'

This drew our attention to other items up there: a blue pot swan with little dried flowers inside, a colourful glass with Blackpool painted around the top and a cream jug from Scarborough.

Suddenly, Lil blurted out, 'Bunion lotion!'

'Lil!' said Kath.

'What's a carbuncle?'

We drank our juice and munched down the biscuits Mrs Mooney had kindly offered to us, then left.

'When's Kenny in?' Kath asked (she was referring to Dad).

'Oh, about 5.30,' I said.

Kath wanted to know if there was somewhere good to play until then, so I took them to Elswick Park. What was known as the 'low park' was on Scotswood Road and the top park ran from Elswick Road through onto Armstrong Road. The top park had more to it – a little pond with steps leading into it where you could plodge (paddle), drinking fountains, sculptures, swings, slides, a tennis court, shuggy boat and much more. The witches' hat roundabout was a lethal weapon. Set in concrete (no safety surfaces in those days), it was a conical structure held up by an iron pole which bobbed about randomly, occasionally crashing into the pole. Lots of kids stood on the wooden plank circular seat, so God help them if anyone's fingers were in line with the pole, or if an absent-minded child was walking too close to it.

Dad was pleased to see my cousins and noted how like Beattie Kath was, but he never made any arrangements to see them again or to visit his sister. On the other hand, I was to spend most of that year's six-week summer holiday at their house at Kinross Drive in North Kenton. It was in a block of flats on the first floor. There was a communal drying room for washing (which was never used) and outdoor lines (again, never used). The house had three bedrooms which were from the landing, as in conventional housing, but the fourth bedroom was enormous as it was above the drying room the same size. Today, the top floor has been removed, the block renovated and sold as private. The green where we used to play is now cordoned off by black metal fencing. It was modern compared to our old Victorian place.

Beattie was lovely; she was lively and always smiling in spite of making a dinner every day, washing, ironing and keeping home for five adults and three children. At one point, she was also catering for her husband's friend Sheff (he came from Sheffield) and the McNally family – husband, wife and baby son – who lodged there for a while, and me, of course.

I could see some eccentricities of my dad in her, but of a much milder nature. She had wanted a new carpet for the landing at the top of the stairs, so she called a salesman to the house. The lad had a large samples book with a wide colour range. Beattie told him that she didn't have time to look through it, but would decide later if he left it with her. After he left, she proceeded to take the book apart and made her own patchwork creation carpet.

A widow with two sons, Alan and Jimmy, Beattie lost her husband James in a mining accident. She was married a second time to John McNamara, whose son Michael also lived with them, plus Kath, Lil and Billy, who came along later.

As Kath was the eldest among us four, she decided the places we went to and the games we played. Trespassers was a favourite: this involved daring someone to pinch a turnip or other vegetable from someone's garden. Kath's role was to supervise. Down by the railway track was where posh houses could be found with huge gardens. Billy and Lil were good climbers, so me and Kath stood at the other side of the fence waiting for the bags of strawberries to come sailing over. We felt a hand grab us on each shoulder and were told to be quiet. When Lil and Billy climbed back, the lady of the house had all four of us captive. She told us off and took the bags away – probably made jam with it all.

Inspired by a deluge of wartime movies on TV, one of Kath's favourite pastimes was to tell Billy that the doctor's surgery was a Nazi interrogation room. The people in there were waiting to be questioned, and if he waited, he would be presented with a medal. Poor Billy sat there, terrified; what must have gone through his mind as person after person went in but didn't come back? Give him his due, as the youngest, he had courage.

Another 'wartime' manoeuvre involved a stake-out at Winthrop's Laboratory. There were always two guards in uniform outside the gates, the fences were topped with barbed wire. Billy was informed that he would be featured on

TV, receive sweets and a medal if he scaled the metal barbed-wire fence, ran to the bottom of the hill and back. This he did and was chased by the guards. He was presented with one of those little silvery Catholic pocket tokens – he always fell for it.

As a Protestant, I wasn't expected to go to Confession while I was up there but went along to St Cuthberts on Balmain Road. Billy stayed with Blackie their dog on its lead in the vestibule while Kath and Lil made their way to the two Confession cubicles.

'What will I do?' I asked.

'Oh, just light a candle,' said Kath, 'and put some money in the box.'

When they came out, I was sitting in a pew with a lighted candle in my hand and wax running all over my fingers.

'What are you doing?' said Kath. 'You're supposed to put the candle on the stand with the others.'

She pointed to the glowing array of lights as she and Lil were laughing.

'You say a prayer for someone who is sick or for someone who isn't here any longer to show that you are thinking of them.'

I stood up and proceeded towards the door with my candle.

'You can't take it with you,' said Lil.

'Why not? I've paid for it.'

'It's got to stay here for the prayer to be answered.'

'But I haven't said a prayer.'

This altercation was interrupted by the sight of the church door bursting open and Billy hanging onto the lead while it was wrapped round a parishioner's leg as she was trying to enter the church. The barking didn't half make a loud echo in the vaulted building.

Blackie used to follow them to church every Sunday – he would wait for a latecomer parishioner to turn up and then he was in. They could see him looking from side to side along the pews until he found them. That dog knew his way all around Kenton, he was as rough as us kids. I replaced the candle and we left the building.

* * *

We also loved trips to Exhibition Park, which had an old bandstand where we took centre stage to sing 'Keep Your Sunny Side Up'. Magazine delivery day was exciting too; they popped through the door with the newspaper. Kath took the *Bunty* and *Judy*, Billy liked *The Beano* and *The Dandy*, Lil chose the *Princess* and *Topper*, I had the *Mirabelle*, but came off well in this as I could read them all. They collected the comics in a huge pile and once more, Kath had an 'idea'. At bedtime, us girls shared a king-sized bed and Billy had his own room. When he was asleep, Kath crept to his door with a bunch of comics, which she placed precariously on top of his slightly ajar door. She shouted for him to come into our room and when he pulled the handle, the comics came tumbling down onto his head. After much panic and screaming, Uncle John came rushing up the stairs.

'Pretend to be asleep,' said Kath, which we did.

One night, she persuaded Lil to put a white sheet over

herself and creep into Billy's room. Again, much screaming, and Kath gave the same instruction. She probably got all of her inspiration from the comics, but one prank resulted in Lil screaming until she was physically sick. This time Kath passed it off as a nightmare. Kath was given a chicken's leg from the butcher's and demonstrated to me how, if you pulled the bone, the claws gripped back and forth. This was amazing to me. I was sworn to secrecy, to tell not a soul. That night when we got into bed, I was instructed to sleep on the outside, pretend to be asleep and Lil to be in the middle. She elbowed Lil, then slowly raised the claw out from under the blanket and pulled the bone. It certainly looked suspicious, with Lil wailing like a banshee and me lying there, comatose. Uncle John came belting up the stairs. He knew something was up and this wasn't a nightmare, but he couldn't prove anything.

We played imaginary games during which Billy requested he be called Oswald. (He would come to regret this.) During an argument we would snap back, 'Well, what are you going to do about it, OSWALD?' and he would fly into a temper. It was an unenviable position to be the youngest in the family.

Bungalows for the elderly were directly opposite Kinross Drive. One day, Kath decided to hold a jumble sale to raise money. We collected old stuff from neighbours and around the district and the sale took place in the laundry drying room. A small amount of cash was raised and Kath divided it up, put it into envelopes, about two shillings each, and delivered it to the bungalows. She also did some 'babysitting' for the Hindmarsh family, who had three children and lived nearby.

They left for their night out and left her a sixpence and nice things to eat. Afterwards, Kath said she wasn't really aware of looking after the children, only that she sat in the house eating crisps and sweets until the couple came back.

* * *

Cousin Michael was the black sheep – he has quite a following in North Kenton and is a kind of cult figure. To say that he knew what the inside of a prison looked like will suffice. He took a job as an ice-cream man in the neighbourhood and often allowed us to sit in the van when he parked it outside, much to the annoyance of the local kids, as we kept setting the tune off and they would rush outdoors only to discover it was a false alarm. Michael was a bad influence on Billy as he encouraged him to play the wag off school to work in the van. He hit on an idea to make money on the side by telling the customers there was no squeezy ice cream left, but he could cut a slice from a block – they received the skinniest piece.

Later, when Kath took up employment for a company in town, Michael asked her what her duties were. He became interested when she said that she took money to Barclays Bank.

'I'll tell you what to do. I will meet you when you have the money, give it to me and tell them you were pushed over and it was stolen.'

'No, I can't do that!' said Kath – and she didn't – but Michael went on to greater and more outrageous stuff. He bought an old railway station near Alnmouth in Northumberland. It had two bungalows built on the land, one of which he turned into a gym. There was a fire pit, which he used to destroy old furniture he couldn't sell at his second-hand shop in Amble. Also, a luxury caravan which never went anywhere and still had the plastic protective covering over the leather seats. A replica Statue of Liberty faced towards the railway line and the village of Alnmouth and a huge set of Snow White and the Seven Dwarves lined the wall.

Michael kept dogs and when he opened huge tins of meat, he tipped them into bowls and threw the cans onto a pyramid of tins. The lane next to his main entrance ran up to the house and lands of a local landowner. There were many disagreements between him and the family and one led to Michael threatening to attend the wedding of this man's daughter on his motorbike with pals in tow to disrupt proceedings. He's been featured in the local newspaper quite often too, not one to bow down to convention or to obey orders from pompous folk. So, when he wasn't off on some adventure or 'away' at the pleasure of Her Majesty, he lodged at Kinross Drive. His business card is titled:

Prince Michael The Bastard
'McNamara of Alnmouth'

Michael held down various jobs, one of them as a seller of peanuts at St James' Park, Newcastle United's stadium, on match days. He enlisted the help of Kath and Lil, who were supposed to decant nuts from a huge box into cone-shaped bags to be sold at sixpence each.

'Hey, pack it in,' he shouted, 'you're eating more than you're packing!'

The block where they lived had a set of stairs up to a first-floor communal landing: three families on one side and three on the other, with the laundry airing room in the middle. Kath sat on the window ledge in there one day with a ball inside a long sock, singing out her song as she belted it against the outer wall: 'Above, below, to the left, to the right…'

Dunk, dunk, dunk, dunk.

She went on for what seemed like an age until a lovely old woman who lived below shouted for her to stop. Kath was mortified as she had never known her to be angry, always so friendly. She ran straight indoors.

* * *

The Sampson family consisted of a mother and father, two daughters and two sons. The father was a rag-and-bone man and came home with all sorts. He took the rags to Benny Sheldon, who had a business behind the Co-op near the Dolce Vita nightclub. We went along to the Sampson's and Kath asked if there was anything we could have and came away with colouring books and the odd toy. He was really generous although the family were poor, like most in the area. Uncle John used to cut the crusts off bread when making sandwiches and he would give them to the grateful family.

The Deakins family was made up of a mother, father, daughter and two sons. They were the first to have a TV on the landing and always invited the McNamara kids in to watch *Children's Hour*. One of Kath's friends, Susan, called for her and noticed that the kitchen window was open to the Deakins' home.

'I'm going to get in there and take a look.'

'No, you can't do that.'

'I'm not going to do anything, I just want to nose around.'

Susan climbed inside then returned to open the front door. Kath just stood there in shock.

'C'mon in, do you want a sandwich? No? Well, *I'm* having one!'

She went back in and came out with a jam sandwich, which Kath again refused.

'Right, well, I'll eat it myself. Come in, man, we're not doing anything wrong!'

Kath was relieved when the door was closed and she could go home. She thought that was the end of it, but later that night, a little Dinky car came through the letterbox. Billy picked it up and was 'brumming' it along the floor when another arrived. It was then that Kath twigged: this girl had stolen some of Thomas Deakins's toy cars. She began to panic and terror-stricken, burst into tears and it all came out. *There was murders on!* Beattie alerted the family next door and the cars were returned. In some ways, it was probably a good thing as any burglar could have easily entered that house, so maybe it was a lesson learned.

Mrs Deakins called one day to offer Kath a blue Airtex shirt – her daughter had a new one. To Kath, this was like gold as every week before the school games lesson, the teacher would ask, 'Where is your PE shirt?'

'I haven't got one, Miss.'

'Stand there and hold your hand out!'

Poor Kath was given the belt every Tuesday and all because her family couldn't afford a bloody blue shirt! She was in the last year of school life and had endured this barbaric practice for most of senior school.

Lil had a scholarship to attend La Sagesse School and after the first day, she asked, 'Mam, what's lunch?'

We referred to 'breakfast', 'dinner' and 'supper' whereas the girls at this school were from privileged backgrounds. Lil felt out of place so she hung around with other scholarship lasses.

During her time there, Lil was never belted for minor things as Kath was at St Thomas More secondary. She was looking forward to cookery lessons and was disappointed that the school didn't offer this. Instead, she was taught Latin, which she hated and never took to. In her first test she got four marks out of one hundred, then eight, progressing to sixteen. Her best friend Janice got the hundred all correct.

Beattie was astounded: 'What's the bloody use of Latin?'

When Lil pronounced the word 'garage' as in 'barrage', Uncle John shouted, 'Here, don't start that in this house!' (In the Northeast we say 'garage' as in 'carriage'. Similarly, there's a saying that if you pronounce 'Newcastle' as if it were spelled 'NewcaRstle', you aren't from round here.)

* * *

The Lackenby twins, Mary and Irene, who lived across the road were our favourite port of call for swapping our meagre possessions with. They had good stuff and we drove a hard bargain. This wasn't the case on one swap, though. Kath had a black doll with long hair and Irene owned a Barbie, which was quite new at the time, but she longed for Kath's doll, winged on and on, and eventually Kath parted with it. Much to everyone's horror, Irene cut all of the hair off and played with it for a while, then said, 'I'm sick of this now, I want my Barbie back.'

So, Kath, always unable to upset folks, accepted the baldy one back!

Mr Lackenby always went up the shortcut towards a local pub on Sunday afternoons, so we waited until he came back, hoping he would be a little worse for wear. He took one look at Kath and Lil sitting there in their matching dresses and said, 'Ah, hello, two sisters,' and gave them a tanner each.

We got into swapping jewellery with the twins. Now, when I say 'jewellery', I mean poppets and bits of broken brooch and bracelets from our side. They also picked up the cut-outs from lids on Andrews Liver Salts to make bracelets, but these scratched their arms. The twins owned little silver metal trinket boxes to keep their 'jewels' in. They also collected rosehips from bushes in the surrounding fields and sold them to Winthrop Laboratory in exchange for cash (they were used for the rosehip syrup made in the factory). When they weren't collecting berries, they enjoyed climbing over the fence to a nearby farm to ride the horses. They were always ready to hold a jumble sale or a concert, for which they charged a small admission fee. When I was sixty-six, I met them again at my cousin Michael's seventy-ninth birthday party at the

Kenton Social Club. I was surprised they weren't running a multinational company, so enterprising were they as kids.

Irene and Mary once visited a house in Rochester Dwellings, where it was reported that a family had a statue of the Weeping Madonna – they were charging a few pennies for folks to come in to witness the tears streaming down the face of the Holy Mother. It turned out to be a severe case of condensation, nothing miraculous about it at all. Another family kept a horse in their flat – Lord knows how they got it up and down the stone stairs!

In the flat below Kath's pal Susan lived an elderly man called Mr Cain, who was noted for inviting children into his home to give them sweets. I went along with Kath and Lil to sample some butterscotch, but when we got inside we were expected to sit on his knee before the sweets were handed over. Back at Beattie's, my mam was chatting and Beattie asked, 'Where have you been?'

'To Mr Cain's house for sweets,' I said, unaware that he was out of bounds. 'He tried to put his tongue in my mouth.'

'WHAT!' they echoed.

There was hell on and it was stated in no uncertain terms that we had done wrong. Looking back, one of the adults should have reported him to the authorities, but no one did that in those days. Once outside again, Lil said, 'You shouldn't have said that, we won't get any sweets now.'

Susan's bedroom window was above Mr Cain's flat and she used to fix a button onto a length of string to continually bash it against his window.

Not being one to give in to boredom, Kath announced that we would call in to the children's section of the local library to play 'Hide the Book'. She chose an Enid Blyton and hid it among countless others.

'Right, go find it!'

When we got fed up with this, unable to locate the copy, she set up another activity. Between the six of us she assigned a shelf each.

'Sort the books into size order. You have this shelf, Irene, you can have this one, Mary, over here.'

The librarians would have had a task and a half after we left.

When Kath was given a bike, she went out riding with Susan. Her sister Nina lived in Whitley Bay and she suggested a ride – over twelve miles away – on their bikes to visit. It was around teatime, five-ish, when they set off and Kath hadn't a clue how to get there. This was not all that surprising, considering she had never been anywhere but round the block on her bike, she simply followed Susan. Nina served beans on toast, which Kath had never tasted before. She thought it was wonderful and ate them every night for ages thereafter. Afterwards, she described to me how the butter melted in with the bean juice.

By the time they left it was pitch-black outside and halfway home, a police car stopped them to say they had no lights on. Instead of waiting until they drove away then getting back on their bikes, the lasses took this to mean they had to push them all the way back. It was almost ten when they returned and Kath's deadline was nine, so she received a clip round the back of the head from Uncle John for that one.

Kath told us stories of her times at school. A girl in her class was called Antoinette, a very grand-sounding name it seemed to us for a North Kenton Secondary pupil. This girl was an expert in the cookery room, making puff pastry, which Kath demonstrated for us and she explained how lots of butter was dotted around, then folded over. She used a fork to make impressions around the edges and we waited impatiently for it to cook. I had never tasted anything like it, amazing!

* * *

We took a trip to the Hoppings, a huge travelling funfair which still takes place every year on the Town Moor, around 1,000 acres of land protected by the Freemen of the City of Newcastle. It originally began as a temperance festival with games and sports, and the fair took up about thirty acres of that space. There were endless rides and stalls, shooting ranges, boxing matches, strip shows and illusion mirrors. As we walked past each ride, a different song was playing: 'It's My Party', 'Walk Like A Man', 'Heat Wave'. People stood against the wall of a cylindrical structure: when it picked up enough speed, the floor moved downwards and folks were sticking like flies against the sides. No, thanks! The cake walk was enough for me. Today, fleets of parked cars take up a huge space, but when we were kids, there was only the odd one or two.

What little spending money we had was soon gone and Lil, Kath and Billy planned on returning to Kenton. I was supposed to be staying there overnight, but as I was in the queue for the fortune teller, decided to stay at the fair for a while longer on my own. Stupidly, I spent my bus fare. I remembered a friend of the McNamara's, Geordie, worked on the Big Wheel, so asked him if I could borrow the fare (I could give it back the next day). Instead, he took me to the Lost Children hut. At midnight, me and one other lad about my age were the only children left.

Neither family had a phone, so when I turned up at home in a police car there was hell on. Mam stumbled downstairs to open the front door, half-asleep. The officer who dropped me off was highly annoyed and said this was clearly a case of severe neglect. At the time, my dad worked with Alan, Beattie's son, and he was on the other end of Dad's temper the next day. It was a stupid thing for me to do, and now, as an adult, when I think of those years – 1963 to 1965, the same time as the Moors murderers, Ian Brady and Myra Hindley – I didn't realise how vulnerable I could have been to any person of their ilk. The annoying thing was that after an hour or two in the hut, Thomas Deakins, the son of the family next door to the McNamara's, popped his head inside and asked if I wanted to go home with him. I was so shy, I said no – I could have avoided all that hassle to the family.

One year, a lass called Joan had an older sister who was a stripper at the fair. We asked her to show us her routine. She flopped about a bit, pretending to take her clothes off, but we weren't impressed. Later, we went to watch her perform, but were turned away:

'You kids can't come in here, you're too young.'

Kath and Lil argued we knew her and were neighbours but

that didn't cut it and we were again turned away. However, there was still candyfloss to be had and it was fascinating to see it swirling around in the steel drum to be circled round a stick. You don't see that now, everything is presented in plastic bags. The flea circus was another amazing sight. We totally believed the fella when he said it took months to train them – we had no idea of the life cycle of a flea. It was all done with mirrors and some of the poor little things had feathers glued to their backs, giving the impression they were performing. Then there was the strongman, the lady with the beard, the funny illusion mirrors and the sheep with five legs, finishing off with greasy chips.

We went home and busied ourselves exchanging stuff on the landing of another pal's flat. I was aware that a song was being played over and over – 'It Might As Well Rain Until September' by Helen Shapiro.

'Who's playing that song all the time?' I asked.

'Oh, it's my sister. Her boyfriend's in the army in Aden and she's missing him.'

'Well, what's all the fuss? She's only got a few months to go!'

'She listens to BFBS as well.'

'What's that?'

'It's the Forces Radio and families can send requests for songs to their lads in the army.'

* * *

Billy acquired a tent from somewhere and he and his mates set it up on the green outside the block. Uncle John was concerned when he asked if they could sleep in it overnight, but came round after much cajoling. But he couldn't stay away from the window, checking and rechecking they were OK, especially around closing time. Some drunken lads came past and one of them jumped on the tent, sending it flopping to the grass. My uncle was in a complete panic and went racing down the flights of stairs to chase them off.

'You stupid buggers, you could have killed someone!'

But when the police came, they found dozens of chocolate bars, pop, crisps, empty wrappers and lots of milk tokens in the tent. They put two and two together as there had been a break-in at Hedley's corner shop that night and so the tokens were returned to the doorsteps. Billy was sent to Borstal for three weeks and though Beattie visited him regularly, Uncle John never went. This had a deep effect on Billy in later years. He returned to school after his stint away and his teacher called him a criminal and a thief. Billy blew up and told her where to go, then rushed from the building. Aunt Beattie was summoned to the Education Committee and it was decided that Billy would be transferred to Kenton Secondary School. This disturbs me: why were steps not taken to help him? He was a good kid, but needed more guidance than his own father could give him. 'Let's just wash our hands of him and pass him over for some other teachers to deal with' seemed to be the attitude. It also impacted on Lil.

Lil and Kath both recalled how Beattie cried during the day and the dreaded memory of when she tried to commit suicide. After dealing with her husband's attitude and wayward stepson, things simply became too much for her. Kath found her and as they didn't have a phone, she rushed over to a family friend, who helped. However, as with most working class women, she simply had to get over it herself.

Uncle John didn't work – he sat in his rocking chair in front of the fire all day, then rushed up the road to The Quarry public house at the first opportunity. Most of the time, he simply got drunk and came home, but on the odd occasion he would act himself with other customers. One day, he took Blackie the dog with him and after one too many, the publican removed his pint: 'Right, that's it, you're barred.' He then looked down at the dog and said, 'Blackie, you have been no bother at all, you can come in here any time you like.'

Billy subsequently became disillusioned with school – the teachers offered him nothing and couldn't see their way to recognising an entrepreneur when they saw one or channelling his energies. At eleven years of age he secured a job in the Bigg Market on one of the stalls, learning how to cut keys for a man called Ken, a friend of the family. He also gave Billy a set of extendable ladders, with which he immediately set about acquiring a customer base in the local area. This meant taking a Friday off school every fortnight and he soon developed a skill for excuses. When the shift was done, Billy laid the ladders up against the first-floor balcony of the flat, climbed up, then raised them over the railings and secured them by way of chain and padlock. This little trade proved very lucrative until a pal of his 'borrowed' the ladders and they weren't returned. He moved on to help Michael on his ice-cream van. This meant two to three days a week off school.

Later, he said, 'Why would I want to go to school when I was earning money? They couldn't teach me anything. When would I need to refer to the Romans in my life, or how much coffee was produced in Brazil? What good would that have done me?'

He then worked for a company called Scott and Stobbs at Marlborough Crescent in town, who sold clothes and shoes. As he knew his way around town, a customer asked the boss if he could borrow Billy to take around the shops to show him where various companies were based. The fella was impressed with his street knowledge as they travelled round in his car and Billy pointed out all of the addresses. This became another sideline for our Bill – his pushbike came in handy as he delivered parcels and was paid for doing so.

Meanwhile, Billy cottoned on to the practice of a church which offered free trips to the swimming baths to local kids in return for their presence in church on Sundays. He hid outside with his mates until the procession emerged from Mass, they joined the queue and enjoyed a splash about with the other conscripts.

The summer holidays always came to an end too fast and I longed for the next half term at school so that I could get back to my cousins.

* * *

I formed a friendship with a lass in the Poplars (each block was named after a tree – the Larches, the Beeches, etc.) called Ann, who lived with her dad (her Mam had died when she was very young). Ann was really trendy, she had a record player and we listened to the 'Wooly Bully' and 'The Name Game' and 'Twenty-Four Hours From Tulsa'. Her dad was very protective of his only daughter and complained about the length of her miniskirts. She had a tartan sleeveless dress which she altered to show more of her shoulders; he nearly had a fit and forbade her to wear it, but she did anyway. She formed a friendship with a teenage married man who also lived in one of the blocks. I had the job of arranging meetings by going downstairs in the block of flats to check if he was outside yet. This went on for some months until the relationship ended and Ann was left bereft.

After one of our nights out at the West End Boy's Club, Ann walked home alone. As she was nearing home someone grabbed her from behind and was intent on dragging her onto a grassed area. Just then a light went on in the kitchen of a ground-floor flat and the man ran off. A couple of weeks later we learned that a young lass had been raped.

Our emotions ran riot at this time. I remember being deeply 'in love' with a paper lad – I knew nothing about him, but obsessed about him day and night. When I knew he was on his round, I hid behind the curtain in my parents' bedroom, peering and wasting away with romantic notions. *Norman!* I wrote his name on countless pieces of paper, wandered along Beaumont Street in the hope of seeing him, but with no intention of speaking to him – this was a totally innocent, unrequited admiration, based purely on looks alone. I would have run a mile if he had even smiled at me.

* * *

Back at Kenton, at half term, Woolworths was a favourite shop of ours and we went up to the Hillsview Shopping Centre with our few shillings pocket money. Billy bought Fry's Five Boys chocolate and we were interested in the perfume, but we called it 'scent' – 5711 was all we could afford, or the cheap stuff in tiny coloured glass bottles. Kath had just left school and decided she wanted to work there but was too afraid to ask so we stood outside while Lil went inside:

'Excuse me, have you any jobs going?'

'Yes, who is it for?'

'My sister.'

'Well, where is she?'

'She's outside.'

'Bring her in then.'

Kath was interviewed and given the position as sales assistant on the spot. For the first time, she had more money than she knew what to do with. She bought some crazy foam and sat on the ledge of the laundry room squirting it to the joyful cries of kids below, who eagerly grabbed it.

That Christmas, Kath had saved her money and bought us all a little tin of sweets. The tree was decorated with lights and when one went off, the whole string had to be tested to find out which one had caused the problem. *The Broons* and *Oor Wullie* were the staple choice for annuals. We loved looking around at the make-up in the Woolworths store. Bourjois Rouge was a hard cake of 'Rosette Brune' with a little powder puff inside a cardboard pot. We looked at mascara in a block, which people spat on and rubbed a tiny brush around before swiping it over their lashes.

After Kath left Woolworths, me and Lil went with her to another interview at a company in Byker, but this time we stood outside. The position was at The Metal Box factory, where she sat with ten others, sorting out the tops for bottles of jam and pickled onion jars. A lad came in and tipped a massive boxful onto the table and they checked for scratches or imperfections. Half an hour in and Kath thought, *Yes, I can do this OK*. The lad came back with another box and once more tipped lids onto the table.

'What's he doing?' asked Kath. 'He's already brought a box in for us to sort.'

'Yes, we do this all day.'

'I need to go to the toilet.'

'You can't go now. I'm sorry, I should have explained,' said the supervisor. 'Toilet visits are only allowed during break time. As you didn't know, you can go this time.'

Kath took this opportunity to go to the office.

'I want to hand my notice in.'

'OK, I will just get your file. That's strange, it's not here. When did you start?'

'This morning.'

'Oh well, that would explain it – it hasn't even reached the cabinet. What's the problem with the work?'

'Well, I can't sit here all day, just checking jar lids.'

By the end of the week, Kath had been through all of the jobs in the factory, but still left.

She made a start at a clothing manufacturer in the city centre – they supplied many of the clothing stores in the city. She was shown into a massive warehouse with rows and rows of ceiling-high products. The owner explained that she would be supplied with an overall, the cost of which would be taken from her first wage. He told her that if a store wanted thirty dozen vests, she would be responsible for finding, bringing them to the distribution point and logging their distribution. She took one look around and thought, *How am I going to find stuff in here?* She collected her coat and went home. And so we had her to play with for the times in between her 'new jobs' for a little longer.

With her new employment status, Kath became more aware of her surroundings. She had always been the tidy one and Lil couldn't care less where her possessions ended up so Kath drew a chalk line down the wall, across half of the bed and along the floor.

'Lil, I'm sick of your belongings and clothes strewn all over the place, keep to your side.'

'Where do *I* go then?' said I.

It was a bit confusing for a while, but the rule didn't last long as it was found to be very impractical.

Kath was beginning to grow up and the adventures would soon be no more. I still think of those times and how it really felt like at last I had a brother and sisters. Kath went on to become a secretary and later, when I caught up age-wise, we both worked as telephonists for GPO Telephones. She was to have twenty-two jobs before finally settling down as an usherette at the Odeon on Pilgrim Street.

CHAPTER FOUR

Bognor and The Beatles

Mr Thompson sported a Clark Gable-style moustache; he owned a car which stood outside the house but never went anywhere. His wife wore flat shoes, had flat hair and a flat chest; she took in clothing that needed alterations and had one friend, Mrs Pearson, who lived across the street. The couple had three daughters. Ann was the youngest, aged about seven, and the favourite. Pat was working, fashionable and had a lock on her bedroom door. Then there was Lillian, the middle child, who wasn't particularly favoured by any of them. Lillian emptied any sweets she might be lucky enough to lay her hands on into her pocket so that no one would ask for one. After cookery lessons everyone stood at the bus stop, sharing their creations. Lillian stood at a distance, basket under her arm, ferreting beneath the plastic cover to eat hers. Food which she cooked never made it home, as she knew she would at least go to bed that night without being hungry. Times were hard and some families simply didn't have enough to eat.

Pat had bought a new Sloppy Joe jumper which Lillian was desperate to try on but was forbidden. While Pat was at work, we went out into the backyard, where Lillian had dragged the dustbin under the window. There was a two-inch gap where the sash window had been left open. I had to hold my hand over my eyes as Lillian turned the bin lid upside down and placed a pouffe, box and stool on top. Was she really going to climb up there? Balancing precariously, she pulled down the sash cord and was in. Coming out the way she had entered, she threw the jumper down onto the yard. Once inside, she tried the garment on, but it was far too long, right down to her ankles. Undaunted, a pair of her mother's dressmaking scissors were produced and Lillian, much to my horror, cut the new jumper to size. Swanking around in front of the mirror, she thought she was it – that is until her sister returned from work. I didn't hang around for this, but no doubt Mrs Nosy Parker would have been there to see the fallout.

I should have known better than to trust in Lillian's judgement on anything. One day, during the school holidays, when she was left alone in the house, she asked me if I would like an egg sandwich. Imagining that this would consist of a boiled egg, I said yes. The coal fire in the sitting room was well ablaze and Lillian fetched a chip pan full of lard. This was placed on the fire until the fat was popping. She cracked the egg into this maelstrom and it spluttered into pieces.

'I don't think that's how it's meant to be done,' I said.

Common sense was not a quality Lillian possessed, which was again evident when she decided to try on a pair of her sister's high-heeled stilettos. They looked fair enough, despite being three sizes too big, but what she did next was totally unexpected: she jumped from one dining chair to the next, piercing all six of the vinyl covered pads. Another signal for me to beat it! I told Mam when I got home.

'Wouldn't you think that after the results of the first one she would have stopped?' she said.

'I couldn't believe it,' I told her, but really, I could.

Lillian was always at the bottom of the pecking order when anything was to be handed out. She pleaded with her mother until the last chance.

'Mam, can I have tuppence?'

'No.'

'A penny?'

'No.'

'A ha'penny?'

'No.'

'A farthing?'

'No.'

'Well, can I take the bottles back?'

'No, Ann's having them.'

Lillian was regularly chased by her mother out into the street and pursued around her dad's car. They were darting back and forth, mother at one side, Lillian at the other, round the back, the front, until Lillian made a dash up the street.

When she came to the next parked car, the dance would continue. Mrs Thompson always gave up first. Lillian and I spent time in the street playing with our tops and whips until her mother had calmed down. The tops were wooden, shaped like a mushroom, with a little metal button on the bottom. We wrapped the string from the whip around the shaft of the top, knelt on it, then spun the top around by quickly pulling the whip. The button got extremely hot while it was spinning so could be used to torture anyone who tried to disrupt the game.

* * *

The first year I was taken to Butlins at Clacton-on-Sea my parents were very excited as we had never been away from home before. Mam took great care to choose her best clothes. Dad took a couple of shirts, with which he never wore a tie (he would roll the sleeves up above the elbow) and a couple of pairs of trousers with turn-ups at the hem. He bought a pair of flip-flops, which he didn't like because they did what flip-flops do, so he took the thickest white elastic and sewed it across the top. Not a good fashion accessory as he didn't wear shorts either. But that didn't bother Mam as she wouldn't be with him much anyway. In an unprecedented move the services of a local dressmaker were enlisted to make me seven cotton dresses. I felt like a princess, with one dress for each day.

We took a third-class train from Newcastle Central station and spent the day in London before catching a train to the holiday camp. Dad put on his cockney accent. We proceeded up a few quiet roads with what looked like office blocks and then, as we turned a corner onto Westminster Bridge, I got the shock of my life to see a sea of men in dark suits and bowler hats carrying briefcases. *Where had they all come from, how had I not heard them approaching?* They were marching like they were on a military exercise – I wonder if the idea for the Cybermen in *Doctor Who* came from sights like this?

I met up with a girl on our dining table: Lorraine from 'Leighton Buzzard, Beds'. We went everywhere together and mostly I was with her parents at the fairground, dances and Beaver Club events. She could never get it that Geordies from Newcastle upon Tyne say 'Man' after a request, such as:

'C'mon, man' (meaning hurry up)

Or:

'Hawway, man' (also meaning come on, hurry up).

And even:

'Harraway, man' (Go on with you *or* I don't believe you).

She continually remonstrated with me.

'Don't call me a man, I'm not a man!'

'It doesn't mean you're a man, it just means man! We say it to everyone, man.'

It's surprising how many Norse and Anglo-Saxon words are still used in the Geordie dialect today, for example:

Hoy (to throw)

Wrang (wrong)

Bairn (child)

Hoos (house).

Although we were on holiday with Dad too, we didn't see

much of him. Mam preferred sunbathing, wearing her latest costume, posing and pretending she was a model, while he was off playing snooker or swimming in the sea. When we were by the pool, she asked me to look over at a man lounging nearby.

'Is he looking at me?' she asked.

'Yes.'

'Go over and tell him not to look at me when your dad is here.'

I didn't understand the significance at the time, but in years to come, I couldn't get over the fact that she didn't consider my recollections as an adult. What would I make of this behaviour? She lived for the moment and although Dad was the one with Asperger's, she displayed more than enough insensitivity as far as I was concerned. She certainly displayed more male characteristics. I have never had intimacy with someone I didn't love, but with Mam, she defied the logic of the Billy Crystal quote: 'Women need a reason to have sex. Men just need a place'. Of course you could say her reason was that she enjoyed it, but somehow, I don't think that was the intention of the message.

One night, Mam took Lorraine and me to see the new Beatles' film, *A Hard Day's Night*. After we left the cinema that evening, Lorraine and I sang about love that can't be bought with money. Mam asked us to play on the swings for a while, she had something to do. The man from earlier in the day walked past and she followed. It was getting quite dark by the time she came back for us, but we weren't bothered as we just swung as high as we could, perfecting the lyrics of the new songs: 'I'm Happy Just To Dance With You', 'It's Been A Hard Day's Night'.

The following year, 1964, it was decided that our holiday camp break would be at Bognor Regis. I had had such a great time with the pal I met the year before, but I was worried there might not be anyone to hang about with at this new camp, so I asked if we could take Lillian. Her parents were approached and much to my surprise, they agreed. We travelled by train, Third Class: there were no corridors back then so you had to sit in a compartment accessed directly from the platform. Dad had used white paint to embellish his initials 'K.E.L' in six-inch-high block capitals on his suitcase. This did not please Mam, who grumbled about it. He justified his actions by saying nobody would steal it. It took ages by train, back then, and she was bored, but Dad had his copy of *Reader's Digest* so he was sorted.

Butlins was good fun. I could go off with Lillian and we joined the Beaver Club, where the Redcoats organised all kinds of activities. I would imagine that most kids didn't see much of their parents – it was a totally safe environment. There were donkey derbies, fashion shows and knobbly knees contests. The bathing beauties lined up for contests wearing swimsuits and high heels, their hair piled high, bouffant-style. I still have a photo of when Dad came third with a partner in a ballroom dancing competition – he always hoped that he could win a free holiday for the following year. Mam wasn't interested in such things – she enjoyed dancing, but considered this style old-fashioned.

The week away from home was over all too quickly. There was so much to do and so much to discover – for instance, the sight of a duck's backside. As I had never seen a duck before, it fascinated me how they fed by dipping their heads. All I could see was the backside and tail feathers. Also, that ice cream could be floated in a glass of lemonade and I could be a latchkey kid in a completely different part of the country.

On our return, I went back to Guides and the girl who had given me the lovely blue skirt passed on a straight skirt with four pleats at the front in a little square shape. I did the odd bit of sewing, but this was too difficult so Mam suggested I take it to Mrs Thompson to alter. When I called to pick it up, she said, 'That will be two shillings.'

Mam went off on one: 'We take her daughter on holiday and the spending money they gave her didn't even cover the whole week. Don't you dare go around with that Lillian ever again or there will be big trouble!'

Of course, I did, but she only ever came to mine when they were out.

* * *

I had a small portable record player with a hinged lid. The arm was held in place by a clip at the side. Me and Lillian decided to dance to the odd few singles I owned, but it wasn't working. Against my better judgement I was talked into allowing her to 'take a look at the plug'. I brought in a screwdriver from Dad's toolbox and Lillian patiently removed the two screws from the two-pin plug.

'I will rewire it,' she said. 'I've watched my dad.'

She removed the copper wire strands from the metal teeth, put them back in the same place, but joined the wires together across the middle. It still didn't work, so we just went outside to play. Later, when Dad came in from work, I lied that a fictitious pal called Alice had tried to fix my record player. When he took the back from the plug he turned pale and told me never to do this again, this was very dangerous. Although he could talk! I could have reminded him of the last year when he rigged up a makeshift aerial when we bought our first TV when I was eleven. Mam was mildly electrocuted when she pulled the curtains back.

Dad enjoyed inventing things and could become quite obsessive, which greatly annoyed Mam. He was concerned about a possible break-in to the house – burglars were everywhere – so he devised a kind of Z-shaped black metal contraption behind the front door. It was rigged up to the doorknob at the front. He could have made a fortune from this, had he patented the idea (this was before the deadlock was invented). He had chiselled two rebates on each side into the door frames. When he turned the knob, which was loosened, the Portcullis thingy snapped into place. Mam hated it.

'What if there's a fire and it sticks?'

'It won't.'

As the front door was of the old-fashioned panelled kind, Dad decided to update it by nailing a sheet of plywood over the top. He painted it pale blue and from the outside it looked very presentable, but I was to undo his good work. A daft lad in the next street was always name calling, so when he started in on me, I gave as good as I got. When he picked up half a brick, I knew that it was time to beat a hasty retreat. I had just made it inside when I heard a *dunk* sound. After waiting some minutes for the lad to leave, I opened the door to find the brick lodged in the plywood and threw it away. Dad came in and assumed some vandal had put their foot through it. I said nothing as he foraged for his pliers in the toolbox. So, we were back with our old front door, but this time with a load of nail holes as decoration. Eventually the door was removed and replaced with a trendier design. Not being one to waste anything, Dad used it as a platform to stand on while painting the staircase walls. He rigged up some planks of wood as a bracket – it looked like a miners' shaft, but did the job.

* * *

The old Victorian house we lived in had attics and was built on a steep slope. From the street there were five stone steps, which also led to the downstairs neighbours' place. Once behind our front door there were another fourteen steps to climb before we were on the level where the kitchen, sitting room and two bedrooms were. The attics were up another set of stairs. It was very spooky up there, with three bedrooms and a bathroom.

The back bedroom had a padlock on it when we moved in and Dad jemmied it open. It was full of cardboard boxes with old stuff inside and the skylight window was painted black. The lock was replaced and things left as they were. I only went up to slide down the banister when I was on my own. But with my pals, I wasn't scared. As we sang 'Halfway To Paradise', we stuck posters of Billy Fury on the walls, which we took from the *Pop* weekly magazine.

I once blocked the sink up while making plaster cast ornaments. It wasn't until I was much older and the houses on the road had long since been demolished that a friend mentioned a man had committed suicide in that house before we had taken up residence.

A huge iron boiler hung from the ceiling in one of the rooms. Quite conveniently, it had two rails on the bottom, which were ideal for swinging on. Me and Sarah, a pal from my class, were taking turns. Unfortunately, on my forward swing, it detached from the ceiling. My hands were still grasping the rails as it hit the floor and I lay there, arms above my head. There was water everywhere – I dread to think if it had landed on top of me. Dad came rushing upstairs and clipped me round the ear. Somehow he managed to stem the flow of water but I was so devastated that he had actually hit me, I rushed downstairs and jumped into bed, pulling the covers over my head.

As usual, Mam was nowhere to be seen. Maybe it had been after one of their fights and she had stormed off to her parents for a week or so. Anyway, it was just me and him at home. Sometime later, he came into the room and said he shouldn't have smacked me but it was because Mam had wound him up earlier. He told me that he had only got hitched to her because she was English (he was generally anti-foreigner) and pregnant with me. *Thanks, Dad!* Then he went on to reminisce about his time spent in the army, how he had enjoyed keeping his kit in order, the places he went to and how he had met a girl called Edith who lived on a farm in a place near Hanover. She had been pregnant when he left to return home after the war, but he didn't go back, like he had promised her.

'She was more my type, I should have married her instead of your mother.'

That would explain the letters I found in his wardrobe. Some were in German, so I didn't understand what they said, but I remembered the drawings of horseshoes and bells beautifully coloured in. One photo showed him sitting among five other Tommys outside a tea van with their metal cups. Dad is the only one looking chipper, the rest of them look positively miserable, which would be expected during wartime, but Dad thrived on the regimentation – oh, and obviously, shagging about with the local women.

A friend of mine, Lena, had a German mother and her aunt translated the letter. It expressed a longing to see Dad and how she was so excited to meet his brothers and sisters when she visited his home before the wedding. Poor lass!

* * *

In another of Dad's 'timesavers' a tube of rubber purloined from the garage where he worked was connected to the gas tap. He bored holes through a piece of metal piping and fixed that to the other end. This was meant to save time lighting the fire.

'All you have to do is set up the grate as usual with coal and sticks, then poke this end inside. Turn on the gas tap and light it,' he explained to Mam, who was holding her head in her hands at the time. He then demonstrated this flame-thrower procedure, which never quite caught on. Mam continued to set the grate alight with matches, put a bleezer in front of it and covered it with newspaper. This was meant to draw air away from the blaze, making it take hold more quickly. Regularly, she left the room and the paper ignited. When I screamed, she re-entered, crumpling up the paper and leaving ash all over the place. Being absent-minded, she would often turn the gas ring on, then go looking for the matches. When the light was finally put to the gas, an almighty whoosh went up.

* * *

One Saturday, Dad had bumped into his brother Tommy while in the city centre and was invited to visit. He took me with him. I didn't know where we were headed and I imagined we were maybe on our way to the coast or a park. So here was another sibling of Dad's that I knew nothing of. Tommy lived in a huge block of flats at Rochester Place in Walker, which is in the east of Newcastle. His wife Violet made us feel at home and as soon as I set eyes on my uncle, I could see the resemblance between him and Dad immediately: they were so alike, they looked like twins. Tommy's daughter June was a couple of years younger than me and his son Tom and elder daughter Margaret were working.

We were treated to a lovely lunch and Tommy had lots of funny stories to tell about his working life. As a young lad he took a job as delivery boy, riding one of those huge iron bikes with a metal basket on the front. He said, 'Mr Hewitt would say, "Just go to Weidner Road" or "Just go to Ferguson's Lane" as if it was a couple of minutes away.' One freezing-cold day, Tommy was told to ride a few miles up to Ponteland. He got halfway there and decided he was going no further. Then he punctured the tyre and went back crying. The boss sent someone else and he was given the job of repairing the tyre with a kit in a little tin box. Tommy was sent to the Swan Hunter Shipyard to deliver some lobster and sandwiches for a buffet, which was to take place in the offices. On the way, he took a little filling from each sandwich to keep him going. On arrival, he was in awe of the size of the ships and cranes, the busy, noisy atmosphere and fell in love with the place. After a chat with some of the workmen, he asked if there was any chance of employment.

'Sure,' one of them said, 'go and ask the foreman.'

Tommy was offered a choice there and then, carpenter or joiner. Carpenter was his choice as he preferred to be aboard ship, where he could lay decks and work on the doors to the cabins. He received the Letter of Appointment and his first ship was the *Petrolicus*. Other vessels which were originally trawlers and had been adapted as minesweepers were being changed back to their original use. This was a time for big orders – there had been so many ships sunk by U-boats and as World War II progressed, they had orders for aircraft carriers and oil tankers, as well as cargo ships, with holding tanks for equipment, machinery, guns and tanks.

'Some of them weighed around 200-odd tons!'

Tommy showed us some brilliant photos of his time served in the army. His last photo before service was taken in the Hydraulic Crane pub (named after Armstrong's famous invention) on Scotswood Road. Tommy and two of his mates dressed in army uniform were raising a glass (he had been drinking Guinness and still has the glass). After time served in the army, he returned to the shipyards, where he worked on HMS *Illustrious* and the *Ark Royal*. One of his favourite photos shows him sitting on a rail at the top of a ship with the *Petrolicus* in the background.

'There were no safety harnesses and only ladders strapped to the ship to climb to the top. We had practically done a day's work by the time we walked the deck and climbed up there. It was someone's job to secure the planks we walked on around the outside of the ship, only two-wide. One day, this hadn't been done and I fell through. I managed to catch onto something on the way down, but there were deaths due to safety issues.'

The toilets system was very unsatisfactory compared to modern-day comforts: no cubicles, just one long one-hundred-hole plank, with a little stream of water running underneath to clear away waste. One foreman was particularly disliked by the men, who nicknamed him 'Nappy Neck'. He was in the habit of wearing a nappy to protect his clean white shirt collar and if any dignitary turned up, he would remove the nappy.

If he turned up to snoop on the men at work, someone gave the alert, 'Quick, Nappy Neck's coming!' This was the signal for all men to down tools and sit on the toilet. Unfortunately, this was the opportunity one prankster would wait for. After crumpling up a piece of newspaper, he set it alight, then sent it down the water trough. He watched the fun as the men had their backsides burned.

Another story, which wasn't told to me by my uncle Tommy, involved the use of sign language. As the whole shipyard was a thundering place, men relied on a set of signals, such as for telling the time. Ten to ten was all digits held up twice. If a man was signalled 'What time is it?' and he had forgotten his timepiece the sign was pointing to the left breast and then his back. This translated as 'Left tit behind', meaning he had forgotten his watch.

Dave Anderson, an old pal, used to work as an electrician on ships when Vickers became part of Swan Hunters and asbestos lagging was used. They weren't aware of the dangers back then and were using it rolled up as snowballs. At the end of the shift, the men rushed up to the gate to catch the 39 or 40 bus. A yard detective was holding his arms out to stop them and said, 'Do you know who I am?' to which a cry from a man at the back came, 'Hey, man, there's a bloke here who doesn't know who he is!'

It's difficult to go past the shipyards and see only a handful of cranes today where there were once dozens and a thriving industry, but that goes for many places in the North.

After our hugely enjoyable afternoon Tommy suggested

we visit Walker Park, which was a big adventure. We played football and I got on great with June. It had been something new to me: a family having actual conversations around the dining table. However, this was to be our first and last visit. The family moved home soon after and Dad didn't bother to find out the address so we lost touch completely.

* * *

Elswick Park was beautiful in the fifties. The drinking fountains had little metal circle-shaped cups tied on with metal chains and we always stopped to take a drink. There were huge rocks which I called 'The Mountains', which we climbed up. Dad would often pinch a plant from the conservatory. Yes, he was all for showing his child a good example.

One of my favourite haunts was the Crown cinema on Scotswood Road, opposite the Vickers factories, but then again, everything was opposite Vickers as it took up most of the road on the riverside. Saturday matinees were so popular that once all places were taken, children were asked to budge up to make way for two on each seat. It was a rowdy place to be. Me and Sarah used to stand up on the seats pretending to ride a horse when the cowboy pictures were shown. Come to think of it, there were only cowboy pictures shown except for the odd *Carry On* film. Some slammed their seats up and down at the exciting chase sequences. It's a wonder we heard any of the dialogue.

'Hawway the good 'uns, hawway the bad 'uns!' everyone shouted out.

If the film snapped and the numbers went up on the screen there was hell on with kids screaming. Empty ice-cream tubs and wooden spoons were strewn everywhere.

The place had been built in the early 1900s and was previously The Crown Electric Theatre, which showed silent movies and also offered vaudeville acts. It had been a grand establishment in its time, but was now known as a rough cinema, but cheap on the door.

But violence wasn't something that just happened in the fifties. An advert had been placed in the *Evening Chronicle* in 1933 for a male attendant:

> *Must be fairly well-built and able to take care of himself. Five shifts per week, includes one day off. Hours 5.45 to 10.45 daily, with Saturday matinee. Wage offered 7 shillings per week.*

Jokes went round that the 'lucky' person to secure the job would be expected to provide his own uniform and pay for a police escort on the day he picked up his wages.

So we went to see *The Three Stooges*, *The Lone Ranger*, *Tom Thumb* and many more. Checks on age groups weren't too stringent back then and one film that I squeezed past the cashier to see turned out to be the cause of nightmares and the screaming abdabs in my sleep for weeks afterwards: *The Night of the Walking Dead*. Zombies came back to life and staggered round the streets, trying to eat folks. Well, that would teach me to watch films certified unsuitable for my age!

Above left: My parents, Ken and Doreen, on their wedding day in September 1951.

Above right: Me as a baby with Mam.

Below: My Uncle Tom (far right) having a last drink in the Hydraulic Crane with two of his pals before they set off to serve in the army towards the end of World War Two.

Above left: Me in an early school photo, looking as if butter wouldn't melt!

Above right: Women chatting at a public wash house in Newcastle in 1955.

Below: This is from a street party held in Benwell in the 1950s before houses in the area began to be demolished, and folks moved away.

Above: A concrete train that was built for us kids in the area. I'm to the left, looking up.

Courtesy of Peter Moore

Below: A tank heading up Gloucester Street. Vickers used some streets in the area as test runs for heavy armoury, and people who lived nearby spoke of having to hold on to the china as everything rattled about!

Courtesy of the West Newcastle Picture History Collection

Above left: The Hydraulic Crane, one of the last pubs that remained on Scotswood Road. Most of the pubs on the road were named after industries, machinery or armaments made at Vickers. *Courtesy of the West Newcastle Picture History Collection*

Above right: The belle of the sideshow causing a stir (and some shocked faces!) at the Hoppings Fair in 1955. *© NCJ Archive/Mirrorpix*

Below left: The Quayside bustling with market stalls selling all manner of items back in 1954. *© Popperfoto/Getty Images*

Below right: A woman with her child down Clara Street in the 1950s. The Metrocentre was later built on the site of Dunston Power Station seen across the river in Gateshead. *© Hulton-Deutsch Collection/Corbis via Getty Images*

Above: A fancy dress party in the area which was judged by Connie Lewcock.

Courtesy of Jimmy Grieves

Below: At Butlins with Mam and Dad.

I had a great time at Butlins as a kid – here's me on the carousel with Mam and Lorraine, a girl I met there, (*above*), then with all the other children on the site (*below*, I'm the little girl in the centre of the photo).

Left: My friend Kath in the back lane of Maughan Street.

Right: Me in the backyard of 22 Buddle Road, with my home-made skirt and home-cut wonky fringe next to Mam's deckchair.

Left: Me (far left) with a couple of pals outside one of the trendy shops in Handyside Arcade in Newcastle in 1968.

Above: My Aunt Ellen (centre) outside the Osram Lamps factory on Team Valley, catching some sun at break time.

Below left: Taken after my friend's wedding reception at the Sporting Arms in Scotswood, which overlooked the cooling towers of the power station across the River Tyne.

Below right: Me in my mother-in-law's garden with my brother David in 1971, not long after he was born.

One of the usherettes had two sons who tried all they could to get hold of her torch. When she wasn't at work one night, they decided to smuggle it into their bedroom. Great fun was had shining it under the bed and around the ceiling until the next night when she was on duty and the batteries were flat. She knew who was to blame and hid it away in future. To us, the usherette had a very glamorous job, parading around, up and down the aisles in a tailored uniform. She got to see all of the films for free, what's not to like? It didn't occur to us that this woman would be paid peanuts, on her feet all night, then late home to bed. Sadly, our entertainment was to go the same way as many establishments of the day and was subsequently used as a Bingo hall five nights a week.

One of the local cinemas, The Grande, was nicknamed 'The Loppy Opera' as there were fleas to contend with. When we went to see Bugs Bunny, we literally came out with bugs! We heard that in the past when the old silent movies were thrown out at the back of the building, lads collected them and cut them into short strips. These were rolled into cylinders, wrapped and twisted at each end like a sweetie. They set them alight and threw them into the communal laundry, causing a smell like stink bombs.

Around then, I became tired of going around with Sarah too, partly because she was always borrowing my stuff and losing or spoiling it. A jumper was returned with a single iron print on the front and my portable record player came back with the arm flailing around inside the case, snapped, and the wires on show. The last straw was my precious Sobell transistor radio, which she said had been stolen from her house. Mam went thumping around to their house and Sarah's mother informed her that she had sought a solicitor's advice and was only obliged to replace the radio. She handed over the cheapest make, which had a very tinny sound. I also saw less and less of Lillian as I began going around with three lasses who were older than me and into records and fashion. I was moving into a new stage of my life.

CHAPTER FIVE

Becoming a Beat and Digging the Bands

Reggie's shop stood on the corner of Buddle Road and Maria Street. He ran the newsagent's and tobacconist with his wife Elsie. The couple had two sons: Johnny, who was older and off doing his own thing, and Peter, who was my age and part of a band called The Bluenotes, who practised in the cellar of the shop. Joe was the guitarist and an excellent musician. Dave Anderson, one of the pals we hung around with, was chatting to the band one day when he stepped back and as he fell, snapped the neck of Joe's guitar. Dave was mortified that he had caused such damage and still talks about it to this day. Joe prefers not to think about it. Lads were desperate to become a member of the band and the proviso was to own a musical instrument so this was naturally devastating. A lad called Tom turned up one day: his instrument had suffered a broken neck, which was held together with a massive nail. He was bitterly disappointed as this didn't cut it to become a band member. I wonder where he got that guitar from?

The Bluenotes played all sorts of genres and we loved to listen to them practise. We would sit on the steps discussing the music of the era, who liked The Beatles better than The Stones and who was in the Pop Parade for that week. A curious practice adopted by lads only was to walk around the streets with an LP under one arm, the cover clearly on show: *Rubber Soul* or *The Rolling Stones No. 2*. Meanwhile, the lasses sang their favourites, usually with a transistor radio clamped to one ear. Of course, I no longer had my lovely Sobell.

Other odd habits adopted by the lads included placing a comb up the sleeve of their shirts and once they discovered the use of sachets of shampoo, they would carry one around to show folks what they would be washing their hair with that night. Vosene was considered OK, but with a strong smell, while Supersoft was the cheapie.

I couldn't afford to be fashionable but I did own a pair of bell-bottom jeans and a duffle coat, which classified me as a Beat. I went around in plimsolls (known as 'sand shoes'). This resulted in athlete's foot and I was sent to the doctor, who prescribed a dusting powder. But I stuck with my footwear of choice and attempted to customise to make it more fashionable. There was a bottle of correction fluid in the house so I painted the ridged toes and edgings around the soles. This caused much hilarity from more affluent kids who lived out of the area, who came to hang out in Benwell, but I didn't care.

Jean, Marian and Brenda were in the duffle-coat brigade too so we sort of gravitated towards each other and we all liked The Stones, so that sealed the deal.

I had known Jean since I was five years of age as she lived opposite in Maria Street. Her mother was very glamorous and worked as a barmaid in various pubs along Scotswood Road, the Cushie Butterfield, Old Hall Social Club and Joan Street Club. When she left pub work, she worked on the bread-and-cake stand in Woolworths. Her dad was an ex-miner: he had been involved in an accident at work and subsequently was less active and had put on a lot of weight. He used to wear a huge woollen overcoat, which stuck out in front of him. One day, he was standing on the corner when a lad from Scotswood shouted 'I am a Dalek!' and in spite of his condition, he gave a good chase and nearly caught the lad. People didn't stand for being the butt of jokes in our area, they had pride. Jean's dad kept a pigeon loft at the Panyards on top of a hill and he offered her brother a shilling to clean it out. Jean used to go along too, but he always said, 'You can't wear that flairy [flouncy] frock in here, go home and put something proper on.'

She loved to shake the seed tin to call the birds back and took great pride in clocking them in after a race. They had a baby hen, which they called Jiffy after Jiffy the Broomstick Man on the *Twizzle* TV show. I can still recall the signature tune.

In Jean's house there was always music: an uncle had a banjo and used to play in a pub in town. He usually carried on the show on the bus home to entertain passengers, bus driver and conductor.

Jean was a flirtatious blonde with a twinkling smile. She looked and acted like Bette Midler. Marian was shy and pretty. Lads fancied her, but she wound up getting pregnant to a wrong 'un called Norman. Brenda was the youngest child in her family with four brothers who were considerably older. As such, and being the only girl, she was brought up very strictly. Brenda was also a brilliant swimmer – she won cups for the school at the Northern Counties competitions. She was tough and no lass would tackle her, no lad for that matter. Helen was always courting some lad or other. She was very beautiful with long black hair, but it was always thick with nits.

Mind you, we all suffered this complaint from time to time and unlike today, when the teacher simply sends a note home to all parents and an odourless foam can be applied, a horrible soap and lotion called Derbac was used back then and everyone knew you had the little blighters in your hair as it stunk like creosote. Mam used to vice me between her legs over a sheet of newspaper and scraped my head within an inch of its life. She thoroughly enjoyed finding and capturing a nit or a 'dickie' (adult louse) so that she could crack it with her fingernail against the comb. My scalp was red-raw by the time she was done. I couldn't wait for her to finish so that I could run outside again.

* * *

There were around fifteen of us standing on the corner outside Reggie's one day when we saw Mrs Dean from along the road rush past us with her pram and young baby, her husband in hot pursuit. He was a squaddie who was always absconding from his barracks. He was shouting at her to come back and hurling abuse. As they passed us, we were saying what a bully he was. He got a couple of more yards, then turned on his heel, elbows out and fists at the ready. We all scarpered to the four winds and didn't come out again until after teatime. When we did, we saw a covered wagon blasting down his street. As half a dozen privates jumped out and manhandled him into the back of the vehicle, a cheer went up.

Nearly everyone from the surrounding streets used Reggie's shop. They had three cats, who all loved to sit on the newspapers, so when you wanted to buy one you had to shift a cat along. We bought a quarter of this and a quarter of that, four Fruit Salad chews or four Black Jacks, a penny Dainty bar or two. I tried Caramac chocolate when it was first introduced, but didn't like that. A lovely bar called Bliss had whole hazelnuts lined up along a ridge of milk chocolate, but unfortunately, it didn't last long and was withdrawn from sale. There were lucky bags, Craven Mints and Merry Maid mints. I loved the sherbet dips, which had a length of liquorice inside, or Flying Saucers, also filled sherbet but sealed within rice paper.

We had our newspapers delivered to the house and I sometimes took a few of them to the local chip shop in return for a free bag of chips. They were put onto greaseproof paper, then wrapped in a kind of roll within the newspaper. If the papers weren't exchanged for chips, they would be cut up into squares and hung by string on a hook in the 'netty' (outdoor toilet). Nothing was wasted.

There were many shops along Buddle Road: a butcher's, cobbler's, Laws Stores, a wool shop and a little general dealer. A woman called Bella had a tiny little place which sold sweets, paraffin, mothballs and all kinds. Sometimes if you were in the shop, she went behind a curtain to have a pee in a bucket.

'Mind, don't you steal anything, I can still see you.'

The Post Office had excellent displays of toys in the window, which you could pay for weekly until Christmas. We rubbed our noses up against the window, playing a game called 'I Bogs'. This meant that you shouted out which toys you wanted. The postmistress was none too pleased to have scruffy kids soiling her window with snot and handprints so we were chased. The red box stood outside and one day, as I approached, I noticed six children holding onto each other in a line behind it. They were attempting to avoid a kid who hung out of his bedroom window, trying to take pot shots at them with an air rifle.

A new family came to the road to set up shop. They moved into what used to be an old Co-op, which sold mainly fruit and vegetables, cheese and other foodstuffs. They were Pakistani, and the first in our area, so inevitably, there was a lot of interest.

Jean was a terror of a lass and she went into the shop asking for tartan paint or stripy thread. One day, we were standing outside looking at the display of fruit and veg through the window. I feel ashamed to say now that we were making fun of a spelling mistake: banana had as many n's and a's in it.

'Bannannannnnna!' we shouted.

I was suddenly aware of a tall person standing next to me: it was Arif, the shopkeeper's son. He just stared at me while eating an orange. As I looked up at him, he spat the pip out onto my cheek. I thought this was hilarious and from then on, we got on like a house on fire. He let us sit on his motorbike, which he kept outside the shop.

It took a little longer for Jean to get on friendly terms with him, partly because of her aggravating nature. She held onto the freestanding bubblegum machine which stood outside the front of the shop, shook it so that the bubblegums bounced around, while singing 'Not Fade Away' by The Stones – she was using it as a maraca. When Arif came belting out of the shop, she threw the machine down and the bubblegums were all over the pavement. Jean took off down the back lane, but he chased after her all the way down Greenhow Place onto Scotswood Road – we couldn't believe that he didn't give up, because Jean could run.

She also madly fancied Dave Anderson, who used to hang about with Bob Barton and Tom Locky. Each time Dave appeared, Jean would scream, 'Dave, Dave, ah, yar gorgeous!' He was terrified of her as she ran after him to grab and cuddle him wherever he went. It was just like a fan chasing The Beatles. But she soon got to know what this was like when a new lad called Phil started hanging around the concrete train where we hung out and he chased her in the same manner – it wasn't so appealing then.

There were no mobile phones in those days so kids chatted

about this and that. Dave talked about when he was a kid and they found a stash of World War II Land Army helmets. He put a large box into his haversack, pretending that it was a radio, and wore one of the helmets. Then he turned the sitting-room chairs on their sides so they looked like the front of a landing craft:

'May Day, May Day, Mother approaching!'

We also used to chat about the latest programmes on TV and if anyone had a set and their parents were out, everyone congregated at their place.

We clanned around the concrete park on Buddle Road. It's possible that the council were put off installing anything of a wooden nature after the swings and roundabout were used on the bonfire so a brick maize was constructed as well as a massive concrete train. My cousin Tom had worked on the structure when he was sixteen. He said that the funnel was part of an old sewer pipe and other parts recycled as part of an environmental project. The whole thing was rendered with concrete held in place with huge wooden frames.

After a really heavy downpour of rain a massive area of the park caved in to reveal a disused and blocked-off air-raid shelter. Some kids went in there, but I was always scared by dark spaces after living in our spooky house, so I didn't venture in.

* * *

Me, jean, Brenda, Marian and Helen went to the Majestic dance hall every Saturday afternoon, dancing to all the latest hits on record, and the resident band, Rue and the Rockets, played. We liked their songs, but they were a bit old-fashioned for us now as they wore gold lamé suits and had quiffs in their hair. Sometimes there were other live bands on and we went along: The Small Faces, Herman's Hermits, The Pretty Things... We thought we were so cool, we used phrases such as 'That's fab' and 'It's groovy'. We picked up the *Jackie* magazine, which gave step-by-step instructions for new dance crazes, and danced around our handbags.

One Saturday, while hanging about outside Reggie's, someone had a bright idea that we should all go camping. There was no mention of tents or sleeping bags, only that we would say we were sleeping at a friend's house for that night. I told my folks that I would be staying at Marian's, Jean and Brenda said they would be staying at mine. Around twelve of us hooked up to travel to our destination. I wasn't listening to where that would be until we eventually arrived in a field – we could have been in Aberdeen for all I knew – but it was actually only a couple of miles away in Lemington. It was the middle of November and freezing cold, pitch-black and lord knows why I agreed to go. Two lasses who weren't from Benwell, but had tagged along with a couple of local lads for the camping trip, decided to go for a walk.

Next thing we knew, police were swarming the field, rounding us up. These lasses had a candle and sought shelter inside a stone bus shelter in the village. They were sitting around the flame when a police car turned up. Of course, they told where the rest of us were. We were taken in vans to the station. The five of us and these two numpties were questioned by a female officer. She didn't believe us when we said that we were just hanging around with mates.

'I know what your sort of girls are. I can have you all medically examined, you know. Tell me why you were there.'

At this I flew off and was shouting she couldn't say that to us, I was going to bring my dad down to see her, how dare she say that! I couldn't speak for any of the others, who were telling me to shut up.

'I hope you realise you all have a police record now,' she snapped, but she didn't carry out her threat of an examination. Not that it mattered to me as I hadn't been up to anything, but I often wonder if that was the reason for the attempts to gag me.

Because us five lived within walking distance of each other we were taken home in the same car. It was about three in the morning and Brenda was first to be dropped off. We sat in the car while the policeman knocked on her door. The light came on and shone through the fanlight, her mother opened the door, took one look at the officer and brayed Brenda up against the wall. The policeman was totally shocked.

'No, Missus, she hasn't done anything wrong, she... Please don't hit her...'

'Never mind you, get out of my way!'

Brenda was pulled indoors and we heard the screams from behind her door. It took the policeman a few minutes to adjust to what he had just witnessed before he finally drove off.

'Where to next?'

He set Jean down at the top of her street and waited until she went in. I knew that Marian would probably get the same treatment as Brenda so I said, 'She's staying at my house tonight.'

When we got to my place I walked up the stone steps and pretended to knock at the door, thinking he would drive off and we could sit in the outside toilet until daytime. But, no, he waited until he saw me actually knock and the light went on in the hallway. Mam was her usual bedraggled, half-baked self at this time in the morning.

'There's a party at Marian's house,' I said, 'and we couldn't get any sleep so we've come here.'

No questions asked, the policeman drove off, doubtless relieved to see that no action was taken. Poor Brenda was kept in for a fortnight and us three got away with it.

* * *

We began going to a boys' club called Grainger Park in Elswick. The building had been an old pub called The Vulcan, which stood on the corner of Scotswood Road. Two older lads, Ernie and Ronnie, ran it. There was a tuck shop, snooker tables, music and a basement hall, with a boxing ring, where local fighters such as Paddy Power trained. No space for dancing, but lots of comfy old chairs, where we just hung out, chatting. The place was closed on Sundays, so it was a surprise to me and Jean to see all of the lights on and the front doors wide open.

One day, we went inside and at the top of the stairs Ernie

jumped out, wielding a knife. We nearly jumped out of our skins. What the hell was he doing? Breathlessly, he explained that they had been sorting some camping gear out for a forthcoming trip, only the two of them in the building. When they turned the lights off, they heard footsteps coming up the back stairs from the lower hall. As all the rooms were checked and secured, they imagined someone must have broken in as they were leaving, so they opened the inner doors and ran downstairs, but there was nobody there. This was repeated half a dozen times with the same results.

'Really?' we said.

'OK, well, you'll see… Come on downstairs to check the place with us.'

'There must be someone there, surely?'

The four of us checked every lock, searched every corner and cupboard, then went back upstairs. Me and Jean stood behind the counter in the tuck shop while Ernie and Ronnie negotiated their way through the snooker tables towards the back of the room and switched off the lights. I could see why Ernie freaked out with his knife. Once more the thump of footsteps slowly ascended, then suddenly stopped at the other side of the door. We didn't hang about for this to happen again!

The club was soon to be moved to Scotswood and the old building pulled down. We went along to see the bulldozers move in. Ernie and Ronnie were climbing on the remains afterwards – a huge pile of bricks, all that was left of our beloved meeting place.

* * *

More changes were looming. My parents applied to a private landlord and secured a two-bedroom downstairs flat on Hampstead Road. Mam's friend Irene made viewing properties her hobby so she was there to pass judgement at the first viewing, much to Dad's annoyance. Not one to be put off by his mutting and tutting, she strode through each room commenting on where furniture should be placed.

It was practice at this time for families to arrange an 'exchange' with another family. If they lived in a three-bed place and wanted to downsize, they more or less arranged it between themselves. One of the officers once explained to me that in a time before computers, when an area was marked for demolition, a map was put up on the Housing Office wall. It showed all the streets and each house was categorised by colours. Pink was for rented properties owned by landlords and unfit for habitation, white was owned by the council and grey was an owner-occupier.

A team of investigators would be sent out to interview the families to assess their needs. Meetings could take from twenty minutes to an hour-and-a-half. This officer noticed that he was sitting on the same red sofa in a few of the houses that he called into. A report had been made to the police that two men were seen carrying a red sofa from a house but he hadn't seen where it was taken to. The next day, at around about the same time, the same two men were carrying the furniture back. The man recognised the lads and asked:

'What's going on?'

'It's our Brenda's stuff,' was the reply. 'She and her man have a really nice home and for a few quid, they lend their furniture to families who are due a visit from the housing officer. There's a bloke on Armstrong Road wants a table lamp and two chairs before two this afternoon and old Tommy wants a pair of curtains. They've been off wor Brenda's windows three times this week already!'

Of course, the officers knew what was going on, but turned a blind eye – they knew of the appalling conditions that people were living in, from crumbling walls and dampness to lots of other problems.

Once the homes were vacated, the joiner, brickie, electrician and plumber moved in to secure the property and gas, water and electricity would be turned off. They knew that robbers would be in there to take piping and boilers away – if someone was still in the flat below, there would be water damage to their place.

A lad called Joe and his wife moved out of their upstairs flat and left a chandelier behind (she had decided she didn't want it). Her husband was pleased as he said it had taken an age to fit it in the first place. She changed her mind, but the lower flat had been bricked up and the door of their place was boarded up. The officer arranged for a joiner to meet Joe at the flat and when they got there, Joe had no ladders with him. The joiner loaned him his bench, but was insistent he didn't leave it behind as he needed it for his job. He left Joe to it and returned after an hour, but all was not good:

the ceiling was down and there was a hole in the floor. The joiner reported back to the office:

'There's trouble at that flat, the ceiling is down and I can't see my bench either.'

'Well, is it an emergency?'

'There's no lighting and we can't see if Joe is still in there.'

The joiner, brickie, plumber and emergency services all turned up. Joe had tried to loosen the chandelier, wobbled and hung onto it. As it came away from the ceiling, he fell through the floorboards to the flat below. He came away with only a broken ankle and no light fitting. I don't know if the bench was OK!

* * *

Hampstead Road suited me fine as it was nearer to the clubs I went to and there was a phone in the sitting room. They didn't apply to have it activated, but we could still receive calls. I was in bed one night when I heard my parents fighting so I stayed put. The phone rang and I heard Dad say:

'You'll have to call back in the morning.'

He shouted through 'Yvonne!', but I stayed where I was, not wanting to be dragged into their arguments.

'Who is it?' Mam asked.

'It's for Yvonne.'

'No, she's asleep in bed.'

I leapt up and pelted into the sitting room.

'It's for *me?*'

'You little bugger! You heard me and pretended to be asleep.'

That was the second and last time I was clipped around the ear.

* * *

The biggest change that affected me was the introduction of the comprehensive system in 1965. Our close-knit community friendships were soon to be split not only by housing, but by the education system. The lads were packed off to John Marlay and the girls to Pendower Girls, which changed its name to Benwell School. It must have been a shock to the system for the established pupils who had all passed their Eleven Plus to have their environment infiltrated by interlopers from a variety of secondary schools in the area.

We were set apart from the start as we were expected to wear navy pinafores with pink-and-white or blue-and-white dogtooth check cotton blouses with roll necks, while 'they' were allowed to continue wearing white shirts, ties and blue skirts. The major disadvantage was that they were already two years into study towards GCE examinations, so separate classes were set up for those from the four or so secondary schools. We were mixed together, but got on well with the girls: we were in the same boat.

There was bullying from some lasses who resented us secondary moderns infiltrating their set-up. Two little sods from a central classroom on the ground floor used to rush out if any of us walked past and would threaten us by waving fists. We simply hurried past, but one day, I jumped out in front of them and growled with my fists up. They ran back inside and never did it again. But most of the bullying was carried out by some of the rougher lasses, who looked on them as snobs. Pranks were played, but not amusing in one case. A lass called Chris, who was very shy and quiet, was terrified of bees. Marilyn caught one and put it inside her desk. When the lass opened it, she fell backwards on her chair and was hurt, but the fear of the bee took precedence and she suffered a panic attack. Eventually it all calmed down and folks got on OK.

I took to the lessons immediately. Everything was magic, all the teachers took their roles seriously and we were treated like adults. In English, we studied *Macbeth*, the first Shakespeare play I had ever heard. The teacher played an LP on an old Dansette, it was brown with cream sides. It was like nothing I had ever heard before. There was plot, tension, drama and excitement, so different to the soaps on television. The way we analysed the characters led to a lifetime of enjoyment of poetry and plays.

After three months we took the same tests as the established pupils to decide which classes we would go to the following year. In spite of being a duffer at Maths, I was placed second in the whole year group (this included the long-time pupils). A meeting was called and the conclusion was 'This child has been seriously misplaced' but really it was down to the dedication of staff and the fact that they didn't allow my lack of skills in Arithmetic to deter me from taking part in the other subjects. I moved into my new class and began studies towards GCEs. However, I still could not avoid the Maths lessons. The teacher could have just left me to my own devices as it was clear from the start that I wasn't able to pick up the simplest of tasks, but she assigned me to Heather, a lovely girl who was way ahead. Bless her, she tried every which way to explain manipulation of numbers, but a cardinal number might be a pontiff in the Church for all I knew! She was patient and kind, but to no avail – I was no further forward from junior school.

Miss Cubit, our English teacher, would sweep into the room and always addressed us 'Good morning, ladies'. Her hair was styled in the Sandie Shaw fashion and we loved to watch her look down at her book so that it swung forwards. When I compare the titles for essays at Atkinson Road, 'The Life of a Penny' or 'A Worm's Eye View', there was no contest. Miss Cubit brought a wine bottle into class, held it up towards the light, described the rainbow colours, who may have used it, what the contents had tasted of, maybe it ended its days on a table in an Italian restaurant with wax built up from a lighted candle? Now this was a teacher!

Biology was so interesting. We were allowed to use Bunsen burners for experiments, we learned about teeth, skin, photosynthesis. Why wasn't this taught in secondary schools? Did they think we wouldn't be able to understand, was it because they didn't want us to? After all, who would man the tills, empty dustbins and sweep up? However, in one lesson, worms were given out to dissect. This was not a problem, but then the teacher said:

'Be careful when using the scalpels, they are extremely sharp. They are used for lancing veins in hospital.'

Now, she had no way of knowing my dislike of the mention

of veins. This was definitely Mam's fault, as when I was within earshot when I was younger, she relished in the tale of her encounter at the doctor's for a blood test. Apparently, the nurse commented, 'That's a nice juicy vein,' and Mam had collapsed into a faint. This horror story stuck with me and even today, I have a phobia – the nurses sometimes lose patience with me:

'Hold your arm straight, your arm isn't broken!'

With the image of Mam's encounter plus the aroma of formaldehyde, I slid from the stool in the lab and hit the deck. I was taken to the sick bay until I came around. I spent a fair bit of time in there as I was experiencing some excruciating period pains. Anadin was handed out and after half an hour, I was back on track. This ailment also came in handy for a reason to be excused from games, something I hated. Being four-foot ten inches, I was no competition in netball and I couldn't be bothered with tennis – hitting a ball back and forth, no thanks! This school didn't offer hockey, which I had enjoyed at Atkinson Road.

Across the road from our building and up a little lane was a sports field. We sometimes went up there to practise the long jump, another sport in which there was no contest, with my short legs. Much to our discomfort us teenage girls were marched over there in our white Airtex shirts and navy knickers. I still can't believe that the teachers allowed this. I ask you, why couldn't we have taken our skirts off when we got there? It wasn't only the embarrassment of passing the general public in my underwear that bothered me, it also carried through to this day. I was passing through the Grainger Market on

Clayton Street when an old classmate from secondary school was smoking outside the Star and Garter pub. He shouted, 'Hello Yvonne, are you still wearing those navy knickers?' I was with the photographer of my last book, *The Grainger Market: The People's History*, and another historian. They must have thought that I was protesting too much as I gabbled the meaning of this comment.

I loved Art lessons. We sometimes took our boards and paper into a wooded area to sit drawing plants. Homework wasn't a chore for this subject.

During a prep session we could work on homework in one of the classrooms. One day, Miss Purdie was supervising and I decided to draw her. I had an hour, so I completed the portrait and took it to Miss Macro, our Art teacher and handed it in. The next day, I was walking along the corridor, enjoying the beautiful cherry blossom trees in quadrangles outside of each classroom. I was just about to step out there to breathe in the perfume of the flowers and thinking how lovely the environment was compared to the grey dirt from industry in Benwell. Miss Purdie grabbed me by the arm and pulled me into the side of the hall, where she hissed at me through clenched teeth, 'Be careful who you choose to draw for your Art homework!'

I didn't mention this to my Art teacher. I had obviously captured Miss Purdie, warts and all. Maybe she had been laughed at in the staffroom, but I kept my homework subjects until after school as a result.

We were given rubber tiles on which we drew an image

and the next step was to carve it out in relief with a sharp tool, ready to use rollers and ink for printing. A warning was given before we commenced that because the tools were very sharp, we should score away from ourselves. One lass didn't heed that warning and gouged a hole clean through the soft tissue between her thumb and index finger. I immediately hit the floor in a faint as her blood scooted out, the poor lass was hysterical and the teacher was trying to calm everyone down as she took her to nurse.

I also loved History. The teacher, Mrs Gray, must have been in the early stages of dementia. Of course, we couldn't know or understand at the time so we sat there smirking as she began to speak and then turned her attention to the way her pen was moving. The girls would start to chatter among themselves out of boredom and soon enough a member of staff would lead her gently from the room to be replaced by someone else. On one occasion in her class, my pal Freda and I were mindlessly amusing ourselves by transposing the first letter of our classmates' names – Kathleen Little became 'Laughleen Kittle', etc. – until we came to Charlotte Finn, which translated into Farlotte Chinn. The poor lass had a big chin and we burst into fits of giggles.

'Girls, please share the joke with the rest of the class!' commanded the teacher from the next room as she rushed into our class.

We were mortified at the thought of sharing this with everyone: our cruelty would be exposed for what it was and the disrespect we had shown to our teacher. Because we wouldn't own up, Freda and I were sent to stand in the corridor until break time, one at each end, so that we couldn't continue our disruptive behaviour.

Miss Pickering was our music teacher and she had a novel way of retaining order. She would put a record on – for example, Peer Gynt's *In the Hall of the Mountain King*. She would pick out any troublemakers before the music began, then went on to explain how Peer Gynt had fallen asleep on the mountainside and nymphs came to nip and pinch him. So, off she went during the crescendo, up and down the aisles, nipping the ones whose cards she had marked!

She played the piano and we stood next to it, one at a time, to sing the scales. There were written music sessions, Every Good Boy Deserves Favour (a learning exercise for the notes of music, E, G, B, D, F), and we also learned how to draw a treble clef and a bass clef. Now I knew that Mr Scott was right when he said of my last school, 'What have these people been teaching you?' This was how it was supposed to be and I loved it.

We sat in the quadrangles and discussed the latest records, 'Let's Dance' by Chris Montez and Chris Farlowe's 'Out Of Time'. And we began to mingle in more as we worked on our needlework samples homework, French seams and Petersham bindings. I made a white cotton blouse with flared sleeves, a fashionable sixties item, but by the time I had finished, it was 'out'! Clothing of the day had really stepped up in colours, styles and the more outrageous, the better. We couldn't believe it when we noticed that Eve Brown's store was stocking Mary

Quant make-up, but then we saw the prices and it was back to Rimmel! We loved her dresses and miniskirts as well and tried to adapt our own clothing to imitate her styles. Levi Strauss jeans were also becoming popular, and our parents couldn't understand why we wanted to wear them, as they were worn by working men.

Halfway through the year, a new lass called Gabrielle joined our class. She was from a children's home and took some time adjusting. It was bad enough for us, but starting there on her own must have been difficult. She reacted by being rebellious and disruptive. There were three Hindu girls in the class and as we were all working, one of them, Parveen, screamed out. It was discovered that her backside-length plait had been chopped in half. During cookery lessons Gabrielle went around reducing the regulos on the ovens, which caused another girl to howl as she saw what had happened to her soufflé. Gabrielle didn't stay at the school long!

One day, the Indian girls treated us to a wonderful display of traditional dance in the school hall. It was amazing! We waited cross-legged and in they wafted, wearing the most beautiful silk garments, which were embroidered and decorated with diamanté. The Hindu music began and it was like nothing I had ever heard before, very exotic and mesmerising. Everything was expressed using eyes, fingers and undulating movements. They thumped on the floor with bare feet, their ankles bound with bands of bells, which added to the beat.

But some of the original pupils were bullied by secondary lasses: because the older pupils wore bowler hats and ties, some of the secondary school girls knocked their hats off or pulled their ties. I still don't understand why we weren't all in the same uniform, a recipe for bullying if there ever was one, to differentiate teenage girls by clothing. However, it was all a settling-in process, mainly arising from feelings of inadequacy and not really knowing what our place was supposed to be.

* * *

Mam was working more hours at the restaurant and when a trip to France was advertised via the school letter, she said I could go. I was thrilled, but a little apprehensive as none of my pals were going, but I was allowed to tag along with a few lasses and Heather was coming, so it wasn't so bad. We travelled by coach and then took the ferry to Belgium, where we were to spend our first night before travelling to Paris; the crossing was calm on the way there and we stood on the deck to watch Blighty fade into the distance. The first night was spent near the Port of Ostend, at a scruffy-looking place up a side street. The rooms were very dull: there was a balcony, but the view was decidedly industrial. Mam had bought me a gift set with astringent, cleanser and cold cream; it was the envy of my roommates and they all tried it.

The amount of pocket money we were allowed and the French prices meant that we couldn't buy anything of note while we were there. A day trip to a lacemaking village was planned and we took a packed lunch from the hotel. I don't think anyone could afford to buy any lace, but it was the most beautiful sight I ever saw – all of these very skilled ladies out in the sunshine, spinning away like spiders. We saw the Bayeaux Tapestry and toured the castle at Chinon – fabulous views, but girls of our age aren't the best at appreciating historical triumphs.

One of the posh girls in our group took a fancy to a French waiter at our next hotel in Blois and was intent on impressing him with her use of the French language. He pretended that he didn't understand her. His name was Max and she insisted on calling him Maximillion in the most sexually charged way. She suggested we sneak out of our rooms after lights out to explore the town, but I didn't opt in. I'm not sure she did either as it seemed to me all a puff of hot air and bravado.

Paris was our next stop and this time the hotel was a little worn but much better than the previous ones. The posh girls were perfectly suited to dining out – they snapped their bread from a side plate. The teachers were mortified when us common lot just shoved the whole thing in. I could hear them muttering how we were showing them up. I certainly didn't appreciate receiving each vegetable on a separate plate and where was the gravy? But we had a little wine with the meal, so that made up for it. I'd only taken the occasional swig from my dad's cherry brandy bottle which he had won in a raffle. Wine wasn't something that was heard of in Benwell.

We were puzzled by the sight of a bidet in the room: why would they want two toilets? One of my roommates suggested that it was to wash our feet in, so this we did until we spoke to one of the more enlightened girls, who soon put us right:

'It's to wash your bum in.'

'Arrgh, no, it's never!'

We didn't admit our feet had been in there and that our plates of meat were thoroughly scrubbed that night – ugh!

The most terrifying experience of the whole holiday was when we visited a gift shop. Once more, the prices were sky-high and one of the girls nicked a massive ornament shaped like the Atomium structure in Brussels (built to celebrate the World Fair, a landmark structure from the 1958 exhibition) – the silver balls were substituted with porcelain golf balls and the stand was the clubs. It didn't fit properly into her bag so she asked a pal to keep it for her. That wouldn't have been a problem but we hit a road block with armed police (there must have been an incident totally unrelated to this theft). We were all green as grass and imagined the gift shop had spotted the missing monster ornament, which they would, of course, and had alerted the police. An almighty panic ensued and the ornament was passed from one person to another in sheer panic. Muggins ended up with it and the thief snapped the golf sticks off to force it into my bag. Everyone held their breath but all that happened was the officer boarded the bus, spoke in French to the driver and hopped back off again. The offending item was dumped at the first opportunity.

The return ferry crossing was a nightmare as the ship crashed around on a violent sea. Our party was 'deck only', the seating was those white plastic seats that you see in ice-cream parlours, and as the ship rocked from side to side those of us who tried to sit found that we slid from port to starboard across the wooden surface, trying to avoid the projectile vomit carried further on the sea spray. One lass had bought a baguette for her parents as these were not familiar in Newcastle, only to see the bloody thing snapped into as many pieces as she careered back and forth across the deck. It was a miserable time, we were all freezing cold. Paris in the spring… Bloody hell, if I'd known this, I doubt that I would have ventured forth!

Back at school, I continued to take French lessons but it wouldn't serve me in any capacity other than to say 'Close the door', 'Pass the pen' or 'There it is', 'Here it is'. It annoyed me that there were feminine and masculine words, but of course, the pupils who had passed their Eleven Plus had already been studying this for two years so I was never going to catch up anyway. Studying at home was out of the question as I was out every night with my pals and argued that I probably wouldn't go back to France ever, so why bother?

The atmosphere at school was so different. There were prep hours where pupils took it as their own responsibility to seek a quiet place in the library to revise. Their parents were most likely university-educated and encouraged their children to study, whereas mine couldn't have cared less. These girls played tennis and wore the white outfits, they lived in the posh houses in Fenham and Moorside. I will never forget when I was getting changed for PE one day. Mam had written my name on the tag of my blouse in Biro. I noticed a girl had a specially embroidered name label in her white shirt and immediately covered mine up.

My pals were working and for all I was enjoying the lessons, the thought of staying on at school for another two years seemed like an eternity. They were working in town and earning money so they went to the Majestic dance hall for the lunchtime sessions. As my school was only a few stops from town, I began skipping lunch and jumping the bus to town for half an hour's dancing. I took a dress with me to change into. Lord knows how I was never late back, but I was always hungry: finances being what they were, I was using my dinner money for the entrance fee.

The mock GCE exams were taken and the results surprised me as I was second top for Language and Literature in the whole year, including the original pupils. My results were excellent in all but, you've guessed it, Maths. But I made a decision I would always regret: I decided to look for a job and give up my studies. In later years, I almost blamed my parents for not stopping me, but it was my choice and they just accepted it. They were probably only too pleased that I would be earning money, and aspiring to better yourself wasn't heard of. Instead, you accepted your lot and didn't step out of the class you'd been born into. It's crazy to think that if I had stayed on, in only a couple of years my chances of a good job would have been greater. The school careers advisory team began to pay visits and I was called in for a chat. She offered me an interview for a butcher's shop assistant or serving at Woolworths and was aghast when I said, 'I don't want to go to either of those places.'

'Well, I'm offering you an interview set up for you, what's wrong with those positions?'

'It's OK,' I said, 'I'm going to find my own work.'

I wasn't the only one leaving school, most of the lasses from the secondary moderns were too. We were each given a massive Bible with our names on fancy labels in the front. Someone started a craze for having it signed on the inside cover and everyone began signing at a gallop, running into classrooms to obtain signatures.

My pal Jess was at Rutherford High School, having passed her Eleven Plus; and she was staying on to study for A levels. She was meeting new pals and also, new lads. A lass from her class went to Mark Toney's café on Grainger Street in town. I went along and was impressed when she ordered a cream cheese and pineapple roll. This seemed very posh to me, cream cheese. I had never heard of it and with pineapple too – all we ever ate in our house was Cheddar or Cheshire. At the time all the stonework of the cafés, shops and buildings in Grainger Town was black until an undertaking to clean up the city took place. These stones were actually beige in colour, and the smoke and grime from industry had blackened them. Well, I never – it looked like a new city!

City it may be, but football supporters call it 'The Toon'. The club's nickname is 'The Magpies' because the team wear black-and-white strips. Supporters and their girlfriends are renowned for going without coats in the middle of winter to show their dedication to the team and how hard they are. Other hardy creatures gracing the 'Toon' were hordes of starlings; they nested and perched wing-to-wing on every available ledge, but this was soon to stop with the newly cleaned up facades. Wires and spikes were fixed to deter them, but even now I think of that throng of chattering birds and the sight at a certain time of the evening when they circled and dropped into position all at once for the night.

I went to a couple of matches with pals. At the first one I attended at St James's Park, I got into a panic as there were far too many people in the stands and everyone surged forwards. Me and a friend were given free tickets to a football match between the two teams at Sunderland's ground, Roker Park, as well, which was quite eventful!

Day trips down to Whitley Bay were popular on Sundays and we hung around the bottom of the ramp across the road from the Spanish City fairground. There were hot dogs, toffee apples and winkles in shells ('Willicks'), sold in white paper bags with a pin in the corner to pick the eye off with, and of course, 'The Laughing Policeman' in a glass box or we could play the latest song on a mini jukebox. Lulu belted out 'Shout', and holidaymakers for 'Scottish fortnight' (this was the last week of July and first week of August, known as such because Scottish holidaymakers would descend on Whitley Bay while the factories were closed for two weeks) were parading around in fashionable gear and I was beginning to notice that my duffle coat and jeans were rather scruffy-looking. So many girls there were wearing slacks in powder colours, flowered tops and sandals. On my return journey with Jean, we stood at the station, looking at all the beautifully painted holiday posters with gulls flying, blue seas and flowers. The ladies were smart on those too – it was time for a change of style.

Back at Jean's house we dug out her mam's catalogue to

order some pale blue brushed cotton trews and white tops. We bought blue sandals with Cuban heels and thought we were top-notch. We even tried begging to use her mam's Green Shield stamps to buy something else to wear, but you needed about forty books for a teapot so that was out.

* * *

My Beat friends who were all older than me were moving towards long-term relationships and becoming engaged, so I was seeing Jess more. One lad, who Jess had fancied for ages, asked her out. His father was the owner of a local milk delivery firm. She was so excited to be meeting up with him for the first time. The plan was to meet outside a shop on the West Road at around seven, then to walk to the West End Boys Club from there. Jess, being an expert at dressmaking, was wearing her latest creation and she had purchased a pair of the new hold-up stockings. As she walked along the road, she saw him standing in front of the shop. He was there early, impressive, but as she approached, one of the stockings fell to her ankle. Being the gentleman, he stood with his back turned in front of the doorway to the closed shop while she pulled it up.

After a couple of weeks of dating, he asked her to his home to meet the parents. Jess always had very strong views – and still does – on politics. She was her father's daughter as he was a strong union man, who was well aware of injustices in the workplace. But she blotted her copybook, as when politics came up for discussion, she gave her thoughts freely and strongly, much to the annoyance of her boyfriend's father. The relationship didn't last long after that.

Another lad called Matt, who she met at the club, was very popular with the lasses and Jess went on a couple of dates with him. We were out shopping in town for clothes and she bought a bright orange skirt and a pair of bright green shoes. She showed them to Matt and he said, 'If you wear those tonight, I will pack you in!'

Not being one to bow down to threats, she did just that and he ignored her.

We went to the Oxford a couple of times a week to dance to the popular songs and the occasional band, always wearing our newly-made clothes. Jess's were tacked, pressed, lined up and perfectly stitched. Mine were done quickly to wear that night, usually puckered, zips on show and one puffed sleeve and one flat, but hey! She knew all about Biba and their designs and would add embellishments to enhance her style. We bought paper patterns such as McCalls, Style and Butterick and the occasional Vogue if we had the cash. Culottes were fashionable and we called into Farnons (its catchphrase was 'Try Farnons First'). We bought a yard-and-a-half of fabric at the department store on Nun Street (so-called as the land was once the site of a nunnery and monastery called St Bartholomews, and an original alley called Nun's Lane is still there).

We didn't need that much fabric as our mini-skirts just about covered the cheeks of our arses. Jess bought orange flowered and I chose yellow. We couldn't wait to get back to my house to cut out the pattern. After half a day's sewing, we tried on the body of the garment only to discover they were cutting us in two! Jess thought of a solution to cut the crotch part out and make them into dresses, but I had another idea: pull the stitches out and cut the crotch further down. It worked, we had our culottes after all. I was totally surprised that I had thought of this – it was the only time in dressmaking that I had saved the day.

Tights were becoming popular, which was just as well as the length of the skirts ensured stocking tops were on show. Marks & Spencer had the best colours, American Tan, Ecru and Sandalwood, but they cost an arm and a leg to buy. We didn't have much money, so we saved up to buy a pair and when the toes gave in, we sewed them up and used nail varnish to stop runs. When we were short of cash, we bought the odd cheap pair from a Quayside Market stall. You had to take your chance as on occasion when you opened a packet there would be three legs or a big hole where the crotch was supposed to be.

After being in town all day window shopping and listening to records in Windows, Jess and I came home briefly to get changed. She washed her tights and hung them near the electric fire to dry quickly. Her sister Diane opened the back door and a gust of wind sent the precious legwear clinging to the bars of the fire. They immediately melted and were clagged all over the front like cinder toffee. Diane thought this a huge joke, so we retired to the back bedroom, where Jess had some clothes laid out on the bed which she was hoping to exchange for some of my cast-offs. Diane popped her head around the door:

'Swapping again are we, girls? I wouldn't care, but it's all shite!'

She was laughing and I thought this was funny, but Jess was furious.

'Go next door,' she said, 'and ask her to play "My Baby Wears Knee Socks".'

'Why?'

'Just ask, it's her favourite song – and that really is shite!'

Diane was only too happy to set up the record player, a Dansette which played multiple discs by dropping one at a time onto the turntable. When the music started up, it was the silliest song I had ever heard, but she loved it and flung herself all around the room. Diane loved the movies and emulated any female star – when she saw Sophia Loren on the big screen, she dyed her hair the same colour. Jess caught her in front of the mirror, twisting hair from her temples; she was pulling it behind her ears.

'What are you doing now?'

'I'm going to have almond shaped eyes like Sophia.'

'You could sit there until doomsday and your eyes won't change shape!'

We did buy the occasional new fashion item but we were keen to try unusual stuff too. We bought white straw effect lace-up granny shoes but unfortunately wore them for the first time to the Hoppings. People were gathered around the Helter Skelter and I fancied a try, paid my money and came belting round the chute. As I hadn't been able to afford a pair of tights that week, I wore my mam's stockings and suspender belt. The belt snapped and everything went south as I hit the cork mat with dozens of people laughing. Rain began falling and soon became torrential, our pure white footwear was mired in the mud and so we tramped home, me with my stockings in my pocket.

Our fashion Bible was the *Petticoat* magazine. Jess bought the first issue, which came with a free pair of false eyelashes, but there wasn't enough glue so she had to postpone her first flutter. We sent off for patterns, which were far cheaper – fur hats, tabards and anything that set us apart – always adding tape or some other feature and wore them to show off at the club. The West End had begun as Dockray House, a club for lads. Mr David Dockray started the venture for his son and pals who had nowhere to meet, so he set up activities in the family home garage in the 1940s. As it became more popular, he opened at Sutherland Avenue in wooden buildings built over an old mineshaft. At first, it catered for footballers, boxers and other interests, such as ciné clubs. Eventually lasses were allowed in and sewing and art groups took over some of the space, but the top interest became the dances. We couldn't wait to get in from school to get changed and off out.

One afternoon I hooked up with Marie, a lass who had been in my class. Her cousin Micky tagged along and was a pain in the arse as he kept asking her for a shag:

'Ah, go on, man, I need to practise on somebody who won't laugh at me!'

'Go and fumble around on someone else!' she argued. 'Anyway, it's not right, doing that with a relative.'

'You won't get pregnant, I will be careful. It's only a problem if you get pregnant. Ah, go on, man!'

She ignored him for the rest of the day, being more interested in fashion, but he still persisted.

* * *

Some years after I left school and it too was closed and demolished, it was reported in the local newspaper that a bomb disposal team were called in as there were dangerous chemicals in the biology lab. On reading this, I suddenly remembered one Monday morning during a lesson when the teacher asked me to accompany her to the cupboard where these huge glass bottles with big stoppers were lined up on shelves. I had forgotten to remove my nail varnish from the weekend and she explained that she was going to take it off with acetone. She removed one of the bottles and held it under her armpit to pour some of the liquid onto a cloth.

'This is what is used in nail varnish remover, so it's quite safe.'

Famous last words if any of that lot had gone up!

CHAPTER SIX

Art, Affairs and Budgerigars

After leaving school I called in to the employment exchange, went for a couple of interviews and was surprised to be asked by male interviewers if I was likely to get married in the foreseeable future. This was done to eliminate anyone who was likely to get pregnant, but what a cheek! On realising my mistake at ducking out of further education, I began studying at Bath Lane College of Art. The room was packed full of students, but after a couple of months and into winter some of them left so we had more space to spread out. Topics were given for homework, we could paint or draw. Miss announced:

'The subject for your homework will be "Summer is a Coming In"!'

One of the lads in the class used to slouch in late, wearing long black jumpers in which he had cut holes in the sleeves so that his thumbs protruded through, thus enabling him to hold his brush with the sleeve still covering his fingers. When he turned around, there was a large appliqué cat sewn on the back, but the head wasn't attached so it lolled over the body. It was a freezing-cold, old building, there was only cold tap water to mix our paints and to wash our hands and palettes. He piped up,

'I'm not doing that, I'm doing "Winter is a Coming in"!'

'You will follow my title or I won't mark your work.'

He threw his chair over and marched out of the room. As the ground-floor window was right near the door, he glared at the teacher through the glass, then spat on the window.

I remember one subject was called 'Triple Fugue'. I had no idea what this meant, but didn't wish to show my ignorance, so I looked it up in the dictionary when I got home. It's a musical term and I interpreted it in a painting inspired by the myth of Andromeda and her mother Cassiopeia, who had boasted of her daughter's beauty, bringing a curse from the nymphs. My painting showed the heroine asleep on a bed, the room decorated with murals and ornate pillars standing in front of three arches. Inside the first arch I painted a baby in the foetal position, the second arch showed Andromeda wearing the same clothes as her sleeping self, which was meant to be the second stage of her life, while the third arch showed the Grim Reaper. There was a fourth arch hidden by a lace curtain – it was meant to be the part of her life yet unknown to her. I showed it to a cousin and he said, 'Divn't make me laugh!'

The lad in our class once more riled the teacher by saying, 'I'm going to do a painting on Triple F*ck!' He was the only one in the group who caused trouble and he didn't last long after that incident.

A poster came to my attention on the hallway notice board: '*Volunteers needed. Can you help the elderly, gardening, decorating, shopping or home visits?*' I didn't want to do any of the first three, so I opted for visiting and chatting.

When they chose my first assignment to be in Gosforth, it meant jumping the number 1 bus into town, then the number 2 out. I knocked on the door of a ground-floor flat near Matthew Bank in Gosforth. Miss Hilda Bone answered, then shuffled back into her sitting room, leaving the door open for me to follow. She was in her eighties, with grey hair in a hairnet, and was wearing a long dress and woolly cardigan. It was a small room, with a standard lamp, lace curtains, two comfy chairs with a tiny wooden table between and a large dining table beneath the window. A budgie and cage set square in the middle of the table on a lacy tablecloth.

What did old people talk about? I wondered. None of my grandparents had survived from when I was eight years old, so I had no reference points. I had brought some commemorative Royal Family stamps – old people like the Royal Family, don't they? After polite introductory conversation, I produced the stamps to which Miss Bone snorted, 'I wouldn't wipe my arse on them!'

From that point, I knew that we would get on. She told

me about her niece who was 'A right snob, telling aal and sundry our name is pronounced Bonee. I mean, where's the apostrophe? It's Bone, plain Bone!'

We laughed some more when I told her about a lass in my class whose surname was Tickle and who insisted on being known as Tickelle.

Every Sunday I took the newspapers, she made cheese sandwiches with Military pickle and we drank tea. The budgie, Billy Bone, was left to roam free, hanging from her hearing aid wire. She'd swat him like a fly, then you'd hear a *wheeee, wheee* noise coming from the aid. She didn't half get in a strop when she had to adjust them. Billy would fly off to the net curtains, leaving little claw holes in the fabric.

I noticed her feeding him one day, pouring a tiny amount of seed into his dish.

'There you are,' she said, 'your dinner.'

I mentioned that you're just supposed to fill up the dish so they can help themselves.

'Ah, nah, he'll get too fat! He needs a little for his breakfast, dinner and tea, or he'll get too fat, man.'

After visiting Miss Hilda Bone for three months, I wondered how Billy had survived, until I watched him fly behind the curtain at the front window. When I took a peek, there he was, up to his little thighs in seed, standing inside a huge Kilner jar with no lid. I didn't mention this to Hilda. She said, pointing to his seed tray inside the cage, 'Look, he doesn't eat much anyway, there's still lots of seed in his dish.'

I took her outside and blew over the top of the seed tray: all the husks flew off. She still didn't understand, but Billy would be OK – so long as she didn't find the lid!

'I've got a lovely cream cake for you today,' Hilda said one day as she greeted me.

As the table was so small, she set down the cheese-and-pickle sandwiches, then did a couple of revolutions with the cake as if deciding where it should go. We ate the sandwiches and drank tea, but I didn't see any more of the cake – until she stood up to take the plates away. The cake was stuck to her arse and as she moved, it fell to the floor, squashed into a huge disc.

I was helpless with laughter, but laughing so much I couldn't explain. She began laughing with me although she didn't know why. She coughed her false teeth out into my bag.

'I divn't like goin' into anybody's bag, will you get them oot?'

I said, 'I'm not touching them!' And shoved the bag in her direction.

We used to spend a little time scanning through the newspapers. I took the *Sunday Post*, *Mail* and *The Sun*. As I was reading, I noticed that Hilda was reading the back page of my newspaper.

'Oh, that must have been painful!' she said.

'What?' I replied, turning to the page in question.

'Malcolm Macdonald rips back.'

It wasn't worth the bother to explain football speak.

* * *

A neighbour from across the hall started to bring Hilda a hot dinner every Sunday: turkey, beef, lamb, always with a lovely selection of vegetables and mash with butter. She waited till the door closed behind her, then shuffled into her kitchen to plate up for two. We enjoyed this treat for some time and it was all I could do not to compliment the lady on the tasty food! The neighbour started to admire a sewing cabinet of Hilda's, always commenting how lovely it was each time she set the food down. Hilda asked me to take it home with me and the dinners stopped soon after.

When I arrived one day, she was very distressed: Billy Bone had gone missing. She suspected he had flown out when she'd taken rubbish to the bin. She decided to place the cage on the path outside to see if he would recognise it and fly back. When he didn't appear, she brought the cage back in and set it down on the table. Next day, she picked the cage up to try once more, and there on the table lay Billy, dead as a doornail. He was probably standing there, wondering where his house had gone, when it was planted on top of him. Hilda swore she would never keep another bird.

* * *

We enjoyed many a Sunday chatting and sharing cheese-and-pickle sandwiches and the newspapers. Hilda continued to delight an impressionable teenager with her tales of the luncheon club. 'I don't know how they can be bothered,' she said of the other diners, 'counting out how many sprouts this one has, or who's got a thicker piece of meat than the other!'

Or the time when I called to be told that a plug on her electric fire was sparking, a neighbour had fitted a new plug for her – 'I could have been gassed to death!'

Reminiscing to a friend a couple of years ago, I related this story and he asked, 'What's Military pickle?'

'I couldn't tell you,' I said, 'I just ate it at Hilda's.'

Later, I Googled it. It was made by Haywards, since taken over by Premier Foods of Bury St Edmunds, who make mixed pickle, piccalilli, gherkins in vinegar, pickled beetroot, strong pickled onions, silverskin onions and red cabbage, but apparently, you can only get Military pickle in China. I can just hear Hilda if she's listening, 'Aa can only get it in China now, what's goin' on? You'll be tellin' me that they're bringin' coals to Newcastle next!'

I continued visiting Hilda even after I was married in 1973 as I moved to Kenton Bank Foot nearby where she lived in Red House Farm Estate. But, I feel ashamed to say that as my married and working life became busier my visits became less and less. The last time I visited her a niece of hers was already at the flat when I arrived. I was appalled that she discussed having Hilda admitted to a care home in front of her. Eventually I stopped going so I assume that the niece carried out her plan.

* * *

On my return from Hilda's one day, I found Mam crying again.

'What's happened now?' I asked.

But I had witnessed the regular arguments for a few years now and had learned enough not to take sides. Dad had got into the habit of taking her to the cinema on Fridays. Mam loved the movies, she imagined she was Gina Lollobrigida or Yvonne De Carlo. (Apparently, I was supposed to be called Michelle, but neither of them could spell it when they went to register the birth, so I got lumbered with Yvonne.) Anyway, Dad must have realised that he could save money if he went to see a film on his own. I saw him blatantly hide the newspaper under a cushion.

'Where's my newspaper?' he asked.

'I don't know, I haven't seen it.'

'Yes, you must have, I put it just here [pointing to the table].'

'I tell you I haven't seen it OR moved it!'

'I don't know, I offer to take you to the pictures and this is the thanks I get!'

He would mutt and tutt so much that eventually she would say, 'Well, don't bother! I'm not going with you anyway.'

This suited him just fine. If I tried to interfere, he took my pocket money back.

Around this time, I was having treatment for a wonky tooth at the dentist's. I thought it was odd that each time I had an appointment, Mam insisted on going with me. A couple of teeth were to be pulled and gas was used so I sat right back in the big black chair, the mask was put over my face and soon I was off to Nod. On regaining consciousness, I experienced the most awful pain and blood was streaming from my mouth.

The dentist shoved some chunks of cotton wool in my mouth and all I wanted to do was get back home, but I had to wait for Mam as she chatted and flicked her hair with Mr Dentist in the waiting room. She began booking in for check-ups – getting her fillings done, no doubt. After a while Mam changed my dentist to another one further along the road, a female practitioner. I found out later that she had indeed been having an affair with him.

Seeing as Mam had stopped having nights out at the cinema, she continued going to a local social club. As I said earlier, there was no chance of her bumping into Dad as he went to the Westfield, on the same stretch of road – which was just as well because I was about to leave the flat to go to a West End club one night when a man knocked on the door: silver suit and quiffed hair. A tad old-fashioned, I thought, for the sixties. I had got into the habit of asking no questions and just accepted this was how things were.

'Is Doreen in?'

'No, she's up the road at the Milvain.'

'Ah, right. Oh, I'll see her there.'

I think she was just past caring what Dad thought. He enjoyed dancing but wasn't too bothered about who was his partner – as long as he could dance, he didn't have to socialise with them as well. Now and again, he also got up on stage to sing. He scribbled the words to songs on old envelopes, he never wasted paper. A neighbour told Mam that his partners changed quite often. She said she wasn't surprised.

One night, Dad had been adjusting the mic before offering

his rendition of 'Quando Quando, Quando', but it wasn't responding.

'What the f**k's the matter with this thing?'

His partner at the time refused to dance with him again.

'He's not using language like that in front of me!'

* * *

Mam and Dad still went on holiday every now and again, always to 'Butlitz' as Mam used to call it. But now her brother – Uncle Les – went with them. When I was younger, she had saved money to make the house look nice as Dad kept most of his money to himself, but gradually, she had tired of conforming to what everyone else was doing so she pleased herself. The holiday camp was neutral ground. Dad was in his element, he didn't mind the fact that in the early hours the tannoy in the bedroom blasted out:

Zip-A-Dee-Doo-Dah,
Zip-A-Dee-A
My, oh my, what a wonderful day!

It drove me nuts when I was a kid, so thankfully, I didn't have to go along once Les was opted in. I was old enough and sensible enough to be left on my own. As soon as they were out the door, I arranged a party. The record player was set up and friends began to arrive, but some uninvited guests also turned up and rifled through the drawers and stole records. One of them sat on Mam's new coffee table. It had thin black legs holding up a rectangular contiboard surface, which was covered with a full-sized picture of a Spanish dancer protected by glass. Of course, the whole thing collapsed and everyone was asked to leave. I made up an excuse to Mam that I had fallen onto it. Luckily, she was more concerned that I hadn't cut myself, but I did feel guilty that she would still be paying for it for the next few months on the chucky.

All of my friends were wearing the sixties-style leather jackets and I winged on at Mam to buy me one. I had seen the ideal one in the window of Swears & Wells on the corner of Grainger Street, a specialist in leather clothing, so we went into town. I tried a gorgeous navy shortie style on and it was ideal. The assistant carefully folded and wrapped it up in tissue paper AND put into a flat box. This was the first time I had seen this done, as usually the shops we went to, the assistant chucked your stuff into a bag. When it was time to pay, Mam produced a Provident order.

'Oh no, we don't take those!'

'Well, can we set up tick?'

'I beg your pardon?'

'Hire purchase?'

This could have been an option until she learned of our address.

'I'm sorry, but that area has been blacklisted by this store.'

The jacket was subsequently removed from the box and replaced on the rail. I still feel the shame of that day, Mam trying to convince her that we were good payers, she could show her proof, as we were ushered towards the exit.

Gutted, I trawled some of the shops who accepted 'Provi's' as they were known. Folks paid back a few shillings a week, which usually took a few years to pay off too. The items were worn out before they were paid for. Eve Brown's on Northumberland Street came up trumps with a lovely turquoise leather. I had to turn half the sleeves up inside as they were far too long, but hey, finally, I had the jacket of my dreams!

* * *

There were lots of adverts in the *Evening Chronicle* and I noticed an agency in Whitley Bay, which catered for mother's helps and nanny positions. Maybe this was my chance to get away from the constant fights at home. I nearly didn't get there on time for my interview as, not being used to travelling by train, I was halfway into my journey when I realised that it was heading in the opposite direction of Sunderland. Always at anything too early, I had managed to jump another train. Anyway, it was unbelievable how this company accepted everything I wrote on the form. I had no experience whatsoever, not as much as a babysitting job, but they rang a family in Manchester while I was there and arranged for me to travel there the following week.

When I got home my mam was heartbroken that I was about to leave, but Dad didn't turn a hair so I packed and was off. My best pal Jess went with me to the station to see me off, no parents. As the train pulled away, I was saying goodbye over the pull-down window at the door when the whistle was sounded. Jess grabbed onto the door in a panic that this was it, I was off. This really upset me and I went to my seat and cried all the way there. Not one person asked if I was OK – I had never felt so lonely than at this time.

I was met at the station by Mr Kendal, a shy man, bespectacled (we would call them 'jam jar bottoms' at home), with comb-over grey hair, who took me back to his large house in the suburbs. I met his wife, who was not much taller than me, with bright red dyed hair and tatted within an inch of her life, with a bright yellow leather coat and orange dress. She was very flamboyant and flourished upstairs, bade me follow and showed me my room. Just then, a little girl of about three years of age slinked in around the door.

'I'll just leave you two to get to know each other, this is Lydia. You'll meet the baby, Joseph, when he wakes – he's having a nap in his pram.'

I looked around the room. There was a single bed and a cot, so I was guessing that Joseph was sharing with me. Large plastic Disney figures were on each wall.

'What's in there?' Lydia asked, pointing to my case.

'My clothes, do you want to see them? I'm going to hang them up.'

But she didn't answer, just climbed up on the bed, pulled a cartoon character from the wall and snapped the hook off. She did this to the others, but I didn't want to check her in case she started to scream and what would they think of me, having just arrived? We went downstairs and she asked if she could brush my hair. I agreed and she began very gently, but then started thumping the brush off my head. A hornet was batting up against the window, trying to get out, and I knew how it felt.

After Joseph woke and we had a snack, Mr and Mrs Kendal announced that they were taking me to the market and supermarket, where I would be doing the weekly shop. I would hail a taxi to return back and put all of the items away. Mrs Kendal explained that I would take the children with me on occasion and her husband would drop and pick us up. The children would sit in the trolley while I shopped. I was to get the children up in the mornings, make the breakfast and take on light housework, maybe with a little cooking now and again.

The next morning, I woke, dressed and took the children downstairs.

'What do you want for your breakfast, Lydia?'

'Cornflakes with milk on, please.'

I made this up and put it on the table in front of her and she tipped the bowl, sending the contents all over the place.

'I said cornflakes without milk!' she growled.

I decided that I had made a huge mistake coming here. I was going to be the maid of all work and didn't want to wait around to iron out any problems, so I told the parents and packed immediately. I knew that the last mother's help hadn't lasted long, but I don't know if this happened to the family often. Mr Kendal took me to the station and I was never glad enough to be returning home. The first thing Dad said was, 'Why are you back here? There's been no trouble since you were gone, I wish you'd never been born!'

Thanks, Dad! In fact, the only reason why there had been no fights was that Mam was depressed at my departure and didn't argue back. How could he say that? I had never got involved in the squabbles. Mam was over the moon that I was back, she must have been very down at the prospect of being alone with Dad in that house, but my desire to be out of there wasn't long in resurfacing. One of the lads, Brian from my local youth club, the West End Boys Club, had signed up for the army and waxed lyrical about longing to get out of Newcastle. *Yes, that's an idea, this could be a way out*, I thought. That weekend, I was off to the army recruitment shop in town, where I filled in the application form and was lined up with an interview and a series of medical examinations.

I went into a room where a fella sat at the table: he looked like a doctor but I was highly suspicious when he asked me to take my top off. He sat on a chair and I was standing in front of him. Wasn't he going to take my height and weight, maybe a blood test, an eye test too? He felt my breasts, then asked me to take my knickers off and lie sideways on the bed. He flicked his fingers on my parts twice, then asked me to get dressed. The next lass to go in was in the waiting room and she had huge tits – I was taking the bet that she would be in there longer than me with my fried eggs.

My hearing was to be tested by another 'doctor' in the next room. A short balding man with glasses perched on the end of his nose and of a nervy disposition, he pushed cotton buds up my nostrils, to which I obviously shouted out in pain.

He laughed hysterically and repeated this half a dozen times. What this had to do with my hearing, I will never know.

The last person I was introduced to was a female officer. I was decidedly uncomfortable with her as she was looking me up and down so I decided not to take this up as a career.

The lad from the club, however, did sign up and Lena, Joan, Catherine and me went to see him off at the station, with his uniform on and a long roll of a case over his shoulder. We all promised to write. He came back on leave a couple of months later and said he hated it – he missed the club and drinking in his local, the Chesterfield. Soon after, he bought himself out.

CHAPTER SEVEN

Last Will and Testament

My pal Jean worked in the rag trade at a huge company called Levine's on Scotswood Road. During the summer I had six weeks' break from college and could still go to our lunchtime dance sessions, but Jean was now restricted to a week's holiday. She asked me one day to ring in to her workplace with an excuse.

'Hello, I'm calling on behalf of Jean Clark. She won't be in today as her grandmother died.'

'I thought her grandmother died last month!' came the reply.

I became flustered and didn't know what to say next so I put the receiver down.

Jean took me into the factory one day. I couldn't hear myself speak, the noise from the clatter of the machines was deafening – this wouldn't be for me. I had considered becoming a nurse but realised that I wouldn't be able to stick a needle into anyone so that idea was out too. I heard they use an orange to practise on as it's a similar texture to skin – no, thanks! But it was the sixties and jobs were easy to get. Teenagers walked into a job for a week, decided it wasn't for them and took on another the next. I would go for interviews, accept the job, change my mind over the weekend and accept another, ready to start the following week.

Much to my shame I recall a little solicitor's office in Jesmond, where I kept an appointment at 4.30 on a Friday. The room was very dark and dingy, the only sound from a grandfather clock ticking in the corner. There was an ancient iron fireplace and a musty smell of old newspapers. The interview went well and they offered me the job as an office junior on the spot to start the following Monday.

'For your first task, I have a pile of letters for other applicants to sign and you can post them. It's to inform that the position has now been filled and to thank them for their time visiting us.'

When I left the building, I knew that I couldn't go back there, a leafy street, nothing else around, no shops nearby. Why had I said I would take it? I should have scrapped the letters and rang them at the beginning of the week to say that I couldn't start, then they could have picked the next girl on the list, but I didn't. I posted them and didn't consider that they would have to advertise all over again.

My first position in town was second sales assistant for Timpson's Shoes in the Haymarket – it was roughly where the entrance to Marks & Spencer is now. Linda was a little older than me, skinny, hardly smiled and spoke slowly as she peered through long wavy hair. There were two Daves who worked in the back of the shop: Dave One was in his fifties, deaf and used sign language, Dave Two was in his twenties. One day, I was trying to understand what Dave One wanted for his lunch as he flapped his arms; I didn't get it. Dave Two interpreted this as 'Fly cake' – I wouldn't have got it anyway as round our way it was called 'Sly cake'. I felt a little guilty until I saw him point at me then cup his hands over his chest. I asked Dave Two, 'What did he say?'

'She's got fried eggs!'

The shop was becoming very busy, so the manager took on another sales assistant. She was assigned shopping for lunches and snacks, but every day she brought back treats for us – sweets, cake, that kind of thing. It was kind of her, but in the end we had to politely refuse.

An American lady swaggered into the place one day, plonked a shoe on the counter and a heel beside it: 'I want you to stick this little heel on here, just like that!' It was the first time I had heard such an accent and I was totally taken with her. Butlins at Clacton-on-Sea and Bognor Regis was my idea of foreign and luxurious. We gazed at her, dressed all in cream: coat, hat with a diamond-style pin, gigantic bag and matching shoes. Dave Two said she could pick it up in fifteen minutes. When she returned, she mentioned that she was interested in a shoe dye. The new lass jumped straight in, offering her a range of colours. To demonstrate the colour she opened a bottle, lost her grip and it bounced from the counter, projecting black dye over our customer's face, coat, hat, bag and shoes. There was hell on! The manager was called. He offered free dry cleaning and she could choose shoes and a bag from our shop. She refused and was taken into the staffroom, where 'a solution was reached' but we weren't informed of what that was.

Money was going missing from the till, coat pockets and purses. As the new member of staff was the only one who had not raised this with the manager, he took action. We were told not to go into the staffroom. He sent her to pick something up – he had crumbled a bit of Reckitts Crown Blue Block into a purse and a few shillings inside as a decoy. He stood outside the room and waited until he heard the tap go on. He found her scrubbing the dye from her fingers and she was sacked on the spot. Poor lass was only trying to fit in, and she was in floods of tears as she left.

We did have other colourful characters to serve. Vivian, a well-known gay icon in Newcastle who ran the Imperial pub, famous for its shepherd's pies, paid regular visits, trying to squash his size tens into stilettos. Lads told us that he had glued a coin to the floor of the pub so that he had a good view of any fella bending over. While I worked at Timpson's, all of three months, my wages financed outings to the Majestic dance hall. (I love to see the young kids who go there today, sitting on the path all around the building, waiting for tickets, just as we did, years ago. It's called 02 Academy now.) Anyway, we saw some good bands there such as Herman's Hermits and The Kinks. I remember when they began singing 'You Really

Got Me', the whole place was jumping, but they only sang one more song when lasses began to storm the stage. There were a few crash barriers poorly placed in between them and the crowd. The band ran off, so that was a washout. One of the lads who went there, I used to really fancy him, but the day he came into the shop where I worked, I ran behind the counter.

'Linda, please will you serve him?'

Well, I was only sixteen!

Our shop was on the ground floor and upstairs was occupied by a bookies. I remember a man who worked there, huge, about nineteen stone, used to stand in the joint doorway covered in sweat and stinking of BO, getting some cool air. He wouldn't move if the lasses tried to get past, so they were forced to squash by him – I always waited around until he went away.

When I think back to age sixteen when such things caused embarrassment, how silly it all was: the opportunities missed, an inability to flirt or show interest in anyone. But this paled into insignificance to the problems and heartache suffered by two mothers in a neighbouring estate in Scotswood. A child of ten years of age, Mary Bell, was responsible for strangling to death two little boys who were three and four years old. She was subsequently charged with manslaughter in 1968. Her mother was seventeen when Mary was born; she was a prostitute who was rarely at home and her father was a persistent criminal. The girl didn't have a good upbringing, but those poor little lads, Martin and Brian, were robbed of growing up and their families were forever in torment.

For two years I worked for a firm of solicitors as office junior and as such, bottom of the Last Will and Testament. John was an articled clerk who had failed his law exams to become a solicitor and didn't us beneath him know it! When his shirts became tatty, he used to send me to Rahman, a tailoring and alteration company on Westgate Road, and I had to ask them to take the collar and cuffs off and sew them back on in reverse.

Back then, wills and codicils were typed up on extremely thick paper, no mistakes could be made and Tippex was out of the question. There were dotted lines on the bottom of the documents and little red stickers; seals were placed next to where the signatures would be. Susan and Harriet were secretaries for the partners, Johnson and Carter. I would check the document through with them and take it to John. He gave me time to return back to the office, then rang through:

'Can you come back here, please!'

At this I would quake, knowing I had done something wrong. He once let me stand there, commanding I tell him what was wrong. I wanted to shout, 'You stupid bugger! I'm terrified of you! Do you think I would make a mistake on purpose?' But I stood there, allowing myself to be humiliated. I had missed the seal stickers off, which marked the place clients were to sign. I wouldn't care, but he had a box of them in his drawer.

He once caught me eating a crisp sandwich.

'I've never heard of such a thing where I live!' he exclaimed.

'Well, they're big in Benwell,' I smiled.

There was another time when I went down further in his estimation. I was using an old Pitney Bowes franking machine which stamped the letters. He brought a letter through.

'Where is Penzance?' he growled.

'In France?' I asked.

'It's in Cornwall! You've stamped it air mail.'

I did the same with a letter to Ashby-de-la-Zouch.

For all his faults John was an extremely efficient and hard worker, but such an enormous snob. Mrs Cowen was well past retirement age – she worked for Johnson, did extra hours without pay, collected his dry cleaning and did his shopping. Her office was on the fourth floor and the lift was directly outside her office. The lift was in the centre of the building with stairs spiralling around it. She made sure that both sliding doors were left open on her floor so that she had permanent access to it. As office junior, I had to take a dish full of cups to the basement to wash up and as she had command of the lift, I walked upstairs to shut the doors and descend to my floor – where I placed the cups – and then down again.

During the time I was employed there, she wore two skirts, which were covered in dog hairs (she kept five white Poodles). Every Christmas, she brought in the chocolates she didn't like left over from various boxes she had received as presents. They were always covered in white glaze after being left out in the open. We couldn't help but think that the Poodles had ferreted around, rejected them and we were bottom of the list. Everyone thanked her – and when she left the room, they went straight in the bin. She often made cakes which met a similar fate. I once took a plate of butterfly cakes in to one of the partners with his afternoon tea and he took a huge mouthful:

'These are delicious!' he said.

'Mrs Cowen made them,' I said as I watched him intently.

He gagged and put the rest back on the plate.

Mrs Cowen always made her own drinks in her room – Ovaltine, Horlicks, Choco-Milk. She brought her mug down to fill it with hot water. The dribbles resembled those wine bottles in restaurants where the candle drips in folds down the outside. I kept a large metal kettle and a teapot in our office and had been making tea for six months when I caught her swishing water around the inside of her cup and pouring it into our teapot. Once I told the others, it was kept in the safe after that!

Part of my job was to search for old documents, wills and deeds, in the cellar. How I hated being in there! There were a few vaults for family possessions such as paintings and large black metal chests. Regular individual cases were put into brown envelopes in numerical order on rows of wooden shelving. There were only two shade-less bulbs, which gave the place a spooky glow. The toilets were also in the basement and I washed dishes in the Belfast sink. Health & Safety would have kicked up, but things like that went on. We used a gas ring on the floor of our office to heat soup on!

Once a week I was sent to the registry office with deeds. I got to know a lad who worked for a solicitor's office in Dean Street, who told me their building was haunted. I said our cellar was probably haunted too, it felt as if something was looking at me. We used to walk up Northumberland Street together and back after the deeds were stamped.

Mr Johnson was always buzzing for Susan to go on a message, interrupting her work, but she was still expected to keep in time with his demands. Regularly, he would forget a deed or papers he needed for a case. On one occasion he was to collect his car before a drive to the station to catch a train to London to attend a very important hearing. He left the documents on his desk. Luckily, Susan went to check his office. We both rushed through town to find his car. Fortunately, she knew where he was likely to park too. He was just about to set off when she flagged him down, waving the documents. But she didn't receive much in the way of thanks. When she informed him that she was thinking of taking a Saturday job to finance the purchase of a car, he wasn't happy. His excuses involved what would people think, his secretary working in a shop? She was not offered a raise in salary although her tasks continued to be well outside of the job description.

The private vaults were in a seriously filthy condition and Johnson sought an estimate from a cleaning firm. When they viewed the vaults, they advised that they were so bad, they would only take on the work if it was at least given a once-over first. Johnson lost no time in delegating this job to Susan and another secretary. They worked down there in terrible conditions for a whole week before the firm would accept the job.

After one particularly fraught day of interruptions, he gave dictation and Susan returned to the office to type up. There were two buzzers on the wall, number 1 for Harriet and 2 for Susan, they were connected to an antique clock with an ivory face and ornate pointers. The buzzer hardly ever sounded from Carter, but Johnson had a poor memory and was always calling Susan back mid-sentence to add something else. After a bin full of letters, and another half hour of constant interruptions, she clambered onto the table and stuffed a wodge of tissue behind her number. A foppish Johnson peered round the door in his pinstripe suit.

'Suuuuusan, didn't you hear me buzz?'

She carried on typing.

'No.'

He stood on a chair, stepped onto the table, pulled the tissue out and then chucked it in the bin.

'Please come through and take a letter!'

She took the letter using her shorthand skills and once more returned to her typing. In less than a minute the buzzer sounded again. This kept up and eventually she leapt onto the table, grabbed the pointers of the clock and wrenched them around and around until they snapped. Johnson appeared just as she was climbing down, noticed her flipped-out face, didn't say a word and retreated back into his office.

* * *

Susan was great fun. We went out in our breaks to Jeavons music shop on Pudding Chare, where she would ask for a record to be played in one of the half-booths. One day, she chose Elvis Presley, who she loved: 'All Shook Up'. She danced to the music, twisting and gyrating down to her ankles, but we never bought anything. The first record I had ever bought was 'House of the Rising Sun', recorded by The Animals in 1964. It was the most amazing song I had ever heard. At first, we thought that, being from Newcastle, they were referring to the Rising Sun Colliery in Wallsend, until we listened more carefully and realised it was actually about New Orleans.

Pudding Chare was popular with drinkers. It joined onto the Bigg Market, that dates back to the 1300s and was probably named after offal and black pudding. Such odd names, but Susan knew of the history and told me that 'Chare' is a North-eastern word for a winding narrow lane, which it was, and 'Bigg' is a form of Barley, not as I imagined to describe the size of the place. There was a pub called the Printer's Pie on the lane and that wasn't named after a dish with meat, it's related to old printing practices. *The Chronicle* offices were nearby and journalists and printworkers drank there.

There were three cleaners at the solicitor's office. One of them, Mrs Black, was the supervisor. She had come into some money and suddenly began talking posh. She came to work dressed in the most luminous coloured clothing, bright oranges and pinks, and wearing huge sets of beads. She was also selling perfume products, which Susan and Harriet bought but they found they couldn't wear it, threw it out and went to Fenwick on Northumberland Street instead to buy more expensive brands. One day, Susan was chatting to her and Mrs Black mentioned a shopkeeper, a Mr Smith. Susan knew him and often popped in to buy the odd bag of sweets. Later in the week, she called in.

'I was chatting to Mr Smith and I mentioned that the cleaner where I worked knew him. He said, "Oh, Mrs Black, yes, I know her."'

Mrs Black was furious with Susan.

'You didn't tell him I was a CLEANER! I don't clean, I supervise them.'

The solicitors recorded their voices onto tapes and their secretaries took the tapes to be played back on Grundig Stenorette T machines. After Susan left for a different job, a new secretary was employed. She was a hard worker, very fashionable and liked to wear bright blue eyeshadow, which covered her eyelids and continued up into the eyebrows. I went down to the basement with the dishes one day and nearly jumped out of my skin: she was washing her face, but hadn't removed the eyeshadow first. She turned around as I entered and her whole face was blue!

The poor lass had a distressing experience in her first week there: she dropped the tape reel on the floor as she was coming back from Johnson's office and it bounced around, unravelling as it went. I can still see her sitting on the floor in floods of tears, attempting to roll it up as it just became more tangled.

* * *

During our breaks we looked out of the window towards Mosley Street. There were many banks, which also stretched to the other side on Collingwood Street, all of them pubs now.

It was sad to see the meths drinkers stagger along, hoping for a handout from passing workers. One poor soul used to pull a piece of rope with a branch from a tree behind him and occasionally stopped to talk to it as if it was a pet dog. Another took an age to negotiate the smallest stretch of pathway, as every time someone passed him he stood to attention against the wall. It was a scary sight to see another, who always balanced by his heels on the path facing the busy traffic, rocking to and fro – we had to look away for fear that he would fall into the path of a passing car. They were all making their way to the Salvation Army Men's Palace for a place to stay for the night – an invaluable service which has since closed down.

We can't know of the suffering these individuals endured but I guess some of them would have returned from service during the war and couldn't come to terms with what they had witnessed. Many couldn't adapt to family life as they considered everyday concerns to be minor compared to what they had been through and had been expected to kill others who had done no personal harm to them. And what if they suspected all of this was done in the name of arms deals or gold to line the pockets of the already super-rich, what then? How do you come to terms with that?

A regular street man called Matty called into the Grainger Market to beg for money. The traders looked after him by sending him for change or messages and in return gave him food or cash. Matty had many nicknames – 'The Count', 'The Penguin', 'The Toff' – all because of his gait. He walked at ten to two, full of importance, and strode out swinging a cane, wearing his trilby hat and waistcoat, his hand in the pocket. At first, he wandered about seeking the odd coin and sometimes sang 'Champagne Charlie' as he danced, doffing his cap if a customer passed on a little change. He brought a jam jar filled with tea and occasionally took a drink and put the cap back on. Over time this practice changed and he began filling the jar with whisky. His story was that his brother had killed their mother and Matty took it so badly, he dropped out of conventional society. Inspectors in the market on occasion were forced to remove him onto the street after he became unreasonable. As the market has fourteen entrances this proved futile as they would pick him up, holding him against their chests, as he kicked out in front, drop him out of one door and he would simply saunter back in through another one.

* * *

There were some improvements to the solicitors' office before I left to start work in a new job. A huge glass was installed between the waiting room and one client, while absentmindedly proceeding to Reception, banged smack into it while smoking his pipe. The whole stem was forced down his throat with a smash. I wondered if John might make the same mistake.

For a short time, I worked as a junior at the Church Board of Finance on the corner of Grainger Park Road and the West Road. It was a huge rambling old house, which I think had previously been a vicarage. A lass called Anne was the typist and we shared a large room overlooking the back garden. The staff were very gentile, all church-goers and very reserved –

all except Commander Vermeyden, who brought his little sausage dog called Captain Vermeyden to work with him. It sat on his desk and he fed it pieces of chicken. He always had a friendly word to say and drank his tea in his room in order to look after the dog.

Anne typed on large sheets of carbon-like paper with little holes at the top. I hooked them onto a Gestetner machine, which had a huge drum. It was thick of ink and constantly had to be re-inked as there were hundreds of documents to go out to all the churches in the diocese. I tried each copy first to check there were no creases by turning the drum once with a handle at the side. When all was correct, I could set the machine away to run them off mechanically. We used every spare space on cabinets, floor, fireplace, etc. to spread out each pile of numbered pages and stapled them together.

At lunchtimes we walked over the other side of the West Road to Carricks Bakery to buy pasties or cakes. Sometimes we called in to the Fish and Chippy on the corner of Wingrove Road but ate them outside as the smell wouldn't have pleased some of the secretaries. At breaks, which were two each day, one at ten and the other at three, we all stood very uncomfortably inside the kitchen in a circle to drink tea from cups and saucers (I remembered not to pour it into the saucer!). There was no conversation, and if anyone tried to introduce a subject, usually about the weather, it was over within two sentences. I once bought a fake biscuit from a joke shop with the intention of improving the atmosphere. Peals of false laughter rang out, but nothing more was said. It wasn't as successful when I placed a plastic dog poo in the centre of the room as they all accused the Commander's little dog.

I gave up on humour after that.

* * *

As I was earning a decent wage, I bought myself a new acrylic blue coat. It was fitted with a Peter Pan collar and I loved it. One cold morning, instead of hanging the coat on the stand, I placed it round the back of a chair, near a block storage heater. It must have been too close as it burned a hole in the fabric. I was really annoyed at myself for doing this, but Anne suggested that I could take the coat to Jackson the Tailor on Clayton Street and they would make another to measure, and they accepted tick (weekly payments). So, off I went after work and it was no problem, my measurements were taken, a date was made to pick it up and I was given a little card to log each payment.

When I picked the coat up and tried it on, it could never be the same as my lovely original as the fabric was in suit material – they couldn't make it in acrylic. I wore it just the same and came to love it, even though it took the best part of two years to pay for it.

* * *

People say that in the sixties, you could walk out of one job and into another on the same day and it was true, so I was off again in search of pastures new. My lack of focus and commitment was disturbing to me and I wished dearly that I had continued with my education to gain some qualifications. My new employment at a travel agent only lasted a month. As junior, I sorted the brochures out into blocks of maybe twenty to thirty and took them on foot right across town to any agent who had run out. They were really heavy, so I quickly tired of this.

Next, I tried an architects' firm. There were two of us juniors. Our job was to print copies of the plans, which were folded, then sent out to clients. We took armfuls of these plans to the Post Office and if it was closed, forced them into the box. We collected sandwiches from Fenwick for fifteen architects plus office staff for their lunches. The fillings were luxurious – prawns, chicken and beef in sauces. I learned how to take a little from each sandwich to make our own. It was a nightmare, taking fifteen mugs of tea upstairs to the third floor, three times a day.

One day, I was summoned by a secretary at the other office to pick up some silverskins for her. I walked along the road, into the building and straight into her office.

'Knock when you enter my room!' she growled.

'Sorry,' I said.

'Well, get out and come in properly!'

She absolutely loved it when I asked what silverskins were.

'My dear! A kind of small pickled onion, people serve them at soirées.'

I didn't know what one of those was either but wouldn't give her the satisfaction of asking. Then again, she knew that.

The postman delivered the usual letters and there was a

package which looked like an LP (album). Lisa rolled it over in her hands and took it into the back room. I was shocked to see her open it.

'It might be The Beatles,' she said.

It turned out to be opera and so she threw it in the bin. She was taking a chance, I reasoned, what about the cleaner? She would see it and enquire if it had been put there by mistake and questions would be asked. But Lisa was none too bothered and sure enough, a couple of weeks went by and nothing was said, so maybe the cleaner did take it home.

* * *

On a night out at my favourite dance hall an old school pal told me that she was a telephonist with GPO Telephones and they were advertising for new recruits. This was the best news I had heard in ages.

The interview was held in a building just off Grey Street. I was asked to speak clearly into a telephone, reading from a sheet, to look up some phone numbers. Then there was a spelling test and I had to place some names in alphabetical order. She asked me how tall I was and at 4' 10", I just scraped through. I was told there and then that I would probably be given a start date by letter as I had completed the tests accurately. When I left the room, I was floating on air. I was particularly excited about this job as there would be extensive training in a classroom situation as well as training on an actual switchboard. I would be part of a huge team and it seemed like a true profession to me.

I began work with around twelve other girls. We completed

four weeks' training, which included practising dealing with scenarios, fictitious towns and numbers, awkward customers and building up our speed. Remember, this was an age before computers so we learned how to fill in a card for each call, which resembled a lottery ticket, stating if it was a transfer charge call, coin box or regular subscriber, and this was how Clerical calculated bills. Everything was recorded in code, so Newcastle became 'NT', Gateshead was 'GD', Humshaugh was 'HH', a transfer charge call was 'XFR' and so on. Tickets were placed in a box at the back of the swivel chair and a couple of runners picked them out to take to the clerical desks in the middle of the room, where they were sorted for the Finance department. The headsets were black plastic, trumpet-style, with a flex and plug. Yellow electrician's tape was stuck around the plug. We were the 'yellow banders', which meant we were rookies. I went home every night elated: there were about three hundred operators and the place was buzzing with friendly lasses.

On my first week 'on the board', I plugged my yellow band into a green bander's position. 'Green' meant seasoned operator and I was to work alongside one called Carol – blonde hair, with around two inches of dark roots, thick heavy glasses and quick as blink. She watched me pick up a few calls.

'Number, please, and what is your number, please?'

'Have you had difficulty dialling the number?'

'Trying to connect you.'

Carol unplugged her headset and answered some calls on an adjoining free board and for my next call, I answered with the stock phrase and a male caller told me how long his appendage was. I was totally shocked, this was not mentioned in training. I gasped. Carol asked what was wrong and when I told her, without batting an eyelid she plugged into my board and said, 'Is that all? I've left a longer one at home!'

The phone slammed down.

'These men get a kick from shocking us, so don't be shocked,' she told me.

In time I was soon to adopt the same tone when they asked what colour my knickers were. I was tempted to say, 'I'm not wearing any', but I stuck to 'Not your business, sad sacks!'

Girls had to put their hands up to go to the toilet – if there weren't more than three colleagues missing from their position, you might be allowed. Then you had to place a yellow card on your seat to let folks know where you were. If it was busy, you couldn't leave until a runner came to replace you and even then, you were not to take your plug from the board until they had plugged in.

Supervisors were behind each twenty or so girls and when busy, would run up and down, shouting, 'Pick up another call, double-book!'

Customers could only dial local places and would go through the operator for locations as little as five miles away. Any international calls were very expensive and were connected through special operators. One girl was sacked for connecting her boyfriend through free of charge on a long-distance call. However, some girls took the risk. One lass sat next to me and said she was selling a hairdryer and would I like to buy it? I tried to beat her down on price and she called her mother from the board to negotiate. She was very posh and the family had once lived in Mozambique, so she held the conversation in Swahili. I got the impression that I was going to be 'done' so I declined the sale. Personal calls were also taboo unless you waited for your break and used one of the three coin boxes in the hall.

As in most big companies you came across the odd deal here and there. One lass made bracelets and necklaces from wooden beads and those who couldn't be bothered to make their own provided her with a lucrative little business. Another lass used a wholesale warehouse to buy polo-neck jumpers, which she sold at £1 each – we all had every colour under the sun and they became a kind of uniform. I remember a tall beefy-looking lass with dyed blonde hair, whose boyfriend visited the odd department store after closing time. The best-quality jumpers were sold in the locker room at knockdown prices; she also had a sideline in pans and household goods – popular with lasses about to be married.

Start and finish times were really odd: 8.21 until 5.12 and 9.26 until 6.12. Woe betide you if you were a minute late. Saturdays, Christmas and Easter holidays were covered and each operator was given set dates for summer holidays, but you could easily swap with colleagues between yourselves. This was done by passing a note the full length of the suites: *Can anyone work Xmas day, from 8.21 until 1.26, and I will work your New Year's Day?* If a girl had an appointment at the dentist and needed to be finished an hour early, someone could work an hour for them at the going rate. This was regularly taken up by lasses who were saving up to get married – a few extra coppers in the bank. The bosses didn't mind so long as shifts were covered.

When I compare how easy it is with Internet access today, it seems such a long-winded affair. I was always hopeless at Maths or anything to do with numbers at school. We were all given a radial number, which was our identity: mine was ninety. We recorded our number on each ticket we prepared and that radial number would be on a huge chart on the exchange wall. It was a kind of graph to show where operators would sit during their day: Directory Enquiries, Faults, Clerical, Emergency 999. I used to stand for ages, plotting where I should be. Half an hour on here, fifteen minutes there, it was all so confusing at first. Miss Bell – we called her 'Ding' – was a senior supervisor and I was terrified of her. One day, she came up behind me as I was cogitating.

'Where are you supposed to be?' she demanded.

'I don't know, Miss,' I whined.

She asked my number, went straight to the line on the graph and took me by the arm to the seat. The boards were very tall, so I had to stand on the bar of the swivel chair to reach the top holes to plug in.

We were all familiar with the child callers.

'Get off the line, there's a train coming!'

Then there were kids who asked for the telephone number of Mr B. Brush. We knew what was coming – 'It's Basil, actually' – a giggle and the phone was plonked down.

(Basil Brush was a fictional fox puppet on children's TV at the time.)

Red telephone boxes were dotted around on street corners. On one occasion a gentleman called from a pit village, complaining the GPO was robbing him of his money.

'I've put my money in and there's nobody in. It won't give me my money back.'

'Have you pressed button B for the return of your money, caller?'

'There's no button B in the box, only button A.'

He went on to accuse the service of misconduct, then all went quiet.

'I'm sorry, pet, I've hung me cap on it!'

Some operators were sent to cover for a year at companies such as the Inland Revenue or other government set-ups. I went to the Social Security offices at Longbenton for a couple of weeks. There were six operators and a supervisor, Mrs Ewing. She was lovely – short, red-haired and very glamorous, with a twinkling smile. She regularly brought an uncooked chicken to work and put it in the oven in the staffroom for her supper back home. Another supervisor who covered for her for a week brought in her plants, which she put on the windowsill behind the board. She visited a few times a day to talk to them.

'They grow better if you talk to them,' she explained.

The first day I was there, I was shown the workings of the switchboard. At around 4pm, I heard a rumbling sound, which built to the point where I thought there was going to be an explosion. I looked at the other lasses and none of them broke sweat.

'What on earth is that?'

'Oh, only around 15,000 clerical staff running for the bus,' said Eileen.

* * *

Directory Enquiries held around seventy books, six for London alone. It was a case of in and out of your chair to fetch a book, then leafing through numbers. Some ex-directory numbers' names were sad to look up because immediately you knew why that person was forced to adopt this service – Mr Titball must have had a hell of a time with naughty kids calling him. We knew how that felt because we were targets too. The 999 position was the scariest: we had to listen to calls when they were put through in case the caller hung up in a panic and we could have the call traced. There were hoax calls, mainly for the fire brigade, and it never ceased to amaze me what some folks thought of as an emergency. A Spanish lady was in hysterics, shouting for the police. I put her through after obtaining her number, then listened in:

'My chickens have escaped, they are running all over the place!'

'This is not an emergency, can you please hang up.'

'It is to me, I want you to send someone to round them up.'

A gentleman from Blyth regularly rang up from a coin box, saying there were armed men firing guns on the cliffs or that flying saucers had landed on the beach. We kept him talking until the police got there, then another voice could be heard:

'Thank you, pet. It's OK, we've got him. C'mon, son, let's go.'

So sad. Some people only rang up just to talk to someone. But the memory of one call never left me. A publican rang to say that he had fallen down the stairs with a tray full of glasses. His groin was spiked with glass and he was about to faint. I managed to get the address and the ambulance were called out. We always came off the line as soon as the ambulance service had taken details and we were never informed of the outcome. I often wondered what happened to the hundreds of people in distress every day who asked for assistance, but we had to put them through and let the services take over.

There were also some cool customers. One day, a very calm subscriber rang 999:

'Emergency, which service?'

'Ambulance.'

I put him through.

'Can you send an ambulance, please. My wife has fallen down the stairs and I think she's dead.'

A man asked for a transfer charge call to North Shields. I rang the number and a lady answered.

'I have a call from Edmund Byers, will you accept the charge?'

'Yes.'

I put him through and she said, 'Hello, Edmund.'

He immediately went off on one.

'That's the village I'm calling from, you silly cow! Anyway, why would you accept the charge for a man you didn't know?'

I became so used to repeating the same phrases hundreds of times a day, I once boarded a bus, plonked the money on the tray and said, 'Number, please.'

The driver gave me a strange look.

'Pardon?'

'Oh, I mean two bob, please!'

* * *

The operators had some great nights out. Some of the girls might be leaving to get married and they received a gift – collections for presents were passed around. We went to hen parties at the Eldon Grill on Grey Street, The Mayfair and many other pubs in town. Hofbrauhaus was a favourite: they served beer in huge steins, which you needed two hands to hold. We stood on the tables and wassailed into the night. They also held daft competitions for free drinks, which seemed like fun at the time. For example, the first person on stage waving a pair of knickers or a bra.

In the cloakroom of the Exchange there were little dressing tables with mirrors, where we could put our make-up on and do our hair. There were cork message boards too and I remember one amusing note pinned to an umbrella case: '*To the person who nicked my umbrella. You might as well have the case!*' It stayed there for weeks.

We all felt really sorry for one of the lasses, who had only been married for a couple of months. As we were getting dolled up for a night out, someone had a local magazine advertising a new restaurant in town, which boasted romantic candles in bottles on the tables. Everyone took turns in looking at the photos of diners and this girl spotted her new husband dining with another woman. In contrast, I was in the staffroom making a cuppa and a lass was sat at the table making a list. When I asked if it was her shopping, she said, 'Oh, no! It's a prenuptial agreement.'

June, who was also in the room, took her to task, but she maintained important things had to be ironed out before entering into such an important arrangement. There was quite a heated exchange and June said, 'Well, if I was going to get married and he asked me to sign a prenup, I would run a mile! That's before you even get started.'

* * *

Telegram workers were being laid off and strikes were endemic in lots of industries on Tyneside: miners, boilermakers, the shipyard workers and we telephonists came out for six weeks. I never went on picket duty but some of the girls were pictured in the *Evening Chronicle* on the march with banners. It soon became volatile with cries of 'Blacklegs!' to those who didn't take strike action. I felt sorry for some of them who had young children and were the only waged person in the home as many men were being laid off in professions around the country. It was a time of enormous strike action, and the bin men were 'out', which left huge mountains of rotting rubbish in the streets. I felt sorry for the proud miners who lined up alongside the

Quayside market on Sundays with boxes to collect donations to help the poor families in the pit villages. I remember one man indignantly striding past without contributing and a miner shouted after him, 'It'll be you next, mate.'

One woman who was the loveliest person was frowned on when everyone returned to work. She went to her job during the strike and her husband was charged and jailed as part of the T. Dan Smith council corruption affair in Newcastle City Council in 1974, where some councillors had been taking backhanders. Smith was later convicted of fraud and sent to prison for five years, and took others with him. John Poulson, an architect and politician, was at the heart of the deals. T. Dan Smith had two nicknames and one of those was 'Mr Newcastle' as he had a vision to turn the city into 'The Brasilia of the North'. Some said that he had destroyed many beautiful buildings but he was also responsible for regenerating the area by clearing the slums. Also known as 'One-coat Smith', he used to run a painting and decorating firm reputed to be economical with its use of materials. Despite this, his firm was used in decorating many council houses.

T. Dan had been brought up in Wallsend (the first defence line of the Emperor Hadrian). He witnessed the dilapidated housing problems first-hand – damp and rat-infested properties which hadn't been updated since the Industrial Revolution. His father was a miner and his mother religious and a socialist so he grew up listening to debates in the home on the conditions of the working classes. After becoming a Conscientious Objector during World War Two, he became a member of the Independent Labour Party, who gained a reputation as agitators. He then became a Trotskyist and eventually gained a seat on the council.

The battle was to demolish Scotswood Road, the vein of the area leading to Armstrong's works. In those days the corner of each street had a pub or a corner shop, chip shop or Co-op: all this was to be torn down and huge concrete flats erected in their place. Cruddas Park was his idea of a 'Brasilia of the North'. He had good intentions and genuinely wanted to improve the lot of the masses, but split communities in the process. Young mothers couldn't allow their children out to play, lifts continually broke down and the stench of rotting food from the rubbish chutes was unbearable.

Further new housing was erected: Noble Street flats, which were worse than the old Victorian slums, and became a no-go area. In the past the rows of terraced housing had gone down towards the river, but in their wisdom the council decided to construct rows of flats and houses across the way. Whenever there was a deluge of rain, it flooded into the homes; they only lasted about fifteen years before they too were demolished. The whole city seemed to be in disarray, with families moving house, building sites and strike breakers.

On return to work most of the strike breakers at the GPO resigned as they were given the cold shoulder. The strike didn't serve any purpose and we sensed the end of the service. We now had Subscriber Trunk Dialling (unfortunately abbreviated to STD!). Customers could dial their own calls and we were needed less and less. I did cover on some new switchboards, but they were changing to more modern versions without the cords and plugs. I still had happy memories, so I moved on to BT offices on the clerical side.

I saw Ding a few years ago in WH Smith on Northumberland Street. Well into her eighties, she was as sprightly as ever. I approached her and said, 'Are you Miss Bell?'

We got chatting and she invited me to her home, where we shared some good memories. A formidable character, she used to come to work on a motorbike and sidecar. Before the GPO, she had served in the army in Malta and been a seamstress, making wedding gowns for John Lewis. This had led her to set up a theatre group from the telephonists for whom she made all of the costumes. On one occasion the lasses were unloading outfits outside a venue. In the boot was a full-sized mannequin dressed as the Duke of Edinburgh, with gold epaulettes, hat, uniform, the lot. The car was stolen and Ding rang the police.

'When you find the car, please don't get a shock if you look in the boot. It's not a dead body, it's a model we are using for a sketch.' She hoped the robber would take one look and flee.

I was to work in a few more excellent places and even up until I am making my Last Will and Testament, there will never be an environment that I loved so much as while working for the GPO.

* * *

My cousin Kathleen called to say that her mam Beattie had died. This was in 1977, the same year my first son was born. I immediately thought of how tirelessly this woman had looked after her family, always with a smile, and how she made us smile too, like the time she asked after Kath:

'Is your friend Imodium coming here today?'

'Imogen, Mam, her name's Imogen.'

Beattie had been the most selfless person I knew and I was so sad to hear of her passing. I rushed down to the flat to tell Dad. He answered the door with wet feet, carrying a towel. I followed him back into the sitting room, where he put his feet back in a dish of hot soapy water, the soap and towel strategically placed. I asked where Mam was and at the same time, wondered how to tell him of this terrible news.

'She's gone up to Beattie's house, she died. I was going to go, but it was the last episode of *Get Some In*,' he replied.

Ever wanted to pin someone up against the wall with your bare hands? That was how I felt, but at the same time I knew that he couldn't help the way he was.

Didn't help, though.

CHAPTER EIGHT

Purple Haze and the Caravan at Amble

When Jess went away to university at Hull, I wondered if I should go to the West End club on my own. I was at a loose end and missing her so I decided to pop in one Saturday as The Junco Partners were playing. In the cloakroom, a lass called Jacky began chatting to me. She was an ex-pupil of Benwell Comprehensive and her mates were Lena, Catherine and Joan. They were into wearing Sta pressed trousers and Ben Sherman shirts. Catherine often loaned her trousers out to her boyfriend, Mick. I couldn't afford any of these clothes but I tagged on with them that night and we became firm friends. Luckily, they were also into dressmaking, and being around the same height and build, paper patterns were handed round five times. Attempts were made to create some form of originality by adjusting the necklines, ranging from round, scoop, V and square to slash. We used seersucker as it was the cheapest fabric, 2/11d (two shillings, eleven pence) per yard. Smaller Newcastle businesses and markets continued to deal in 'old money' long after decimalisation and even today, you can ask for a quarter or a half pound of this and that and they will know what you mean and don't put folks right.

I was still cutting corners in sewing stuff up and using giant stitches when the club invested in disco lights, which were luminous. The club management hadn't quite cracked the intensity levels so all of my massive dodgy hemline stitches showed up through the material! It was quite comical at first until the lights were adjusted to be less glaring. As tights were still in their infancy, lasses often paired up an old stocking with a new one. This gave the result of one white leg (the stocking which had been washed often) and one brown leg. Lazy lasses who had only washed the feet of their stockings resembled a Shire horse as the feet glowed due to washing powder remains. Bras could be seen through thin dresses, also streaks in make-up and talcum powder sprinkled on hair for those who couldn't be arsed to wash it. It all glowed like we were in some kind of nuclear power plant.

Joan's family were of Irish descent and on visits to her home, The Dubliners would be playing, except on Thursdays when *Top of the Pops* was on TV. As nothing could be recorded back then, we all sat glued to the screen so as not to miss anything. Joan was working for a solicitor's but went for an interview on Friday, got the job and began work as a trainee punch card operator at the Ministry of Social Security that following Monday. The wages were twice what I was getting, with luncheon vouchers every day. Lena and Catherine also worked there. Catherine used to save up her vouchers and even paid for the drinks at her sister's wedding with them. To this day I still don't know why I didn't apply for work there as the wages and conditions were so good and I missed out on all the chats too.

Under-eighteens were given day release on Mondays when they went to Bath Lane College for Maths and English and took up country dancing and sewing at the YMCA building on the corner of Blackett Street. There were even special buses to take them to work. Catherine had trained as a shorthand typist at school so this would put her in good stead to become an operator at the Ministry in Block A, the only modern building at the time as everyone else worked from prefabricated huts.

The Ministry was responsible for family allowance details, tax deductions, transfers, change of addresses, finances, etc. In an age before computers, workers flicked through stacks of cards. Mistakes were made of course as lasses 'flicked one, missed one, chatted through one', but they were picked up by checkers so no stress there. They punched holes into the cards, the codes were read and fed through a printer. The lasses told me that they were trained by a blind man of around thirty years of age. Paper was placed over the keys of their Olivetti typewriters so they could touch type and if anyone was tempted to look underneath, somehow he knew and would comment.

I smile when I remember Catherine's stories of her family.

Her great aunts and uncle all lived together on Mill Lane and thought that TV presenters could see them through the screen. They never passed each other a sandwich without a plate – 'What would the man think of them?' They waited for the Test Card to appear, then said 'Good night'. They always gave Christmas presents to Catherine and her siblings in June: five shiny pennies, an apple, orange, sweets and a hand-me-down dress for Catherine and her sister, a size 14! One of the aunts made up salmon paste sandwiches and biscuits and brought them every Tuesday. Her Uncle Tommy sold newspapers on the corner of the street, calling out '*News of the World, Sunday Sun!*'

It was round about this time that I met Ron. He had two very popular older brothers who were dressed in the top fashions, with hairstyles like the Small Faces band. It was usually the lasses who got up on the dance floor, but Ron loved dancing too. He seemed a tad effeminate, but we got on really well and began meeting up at the club. One Saturday night, a new band came to play and Ron and I began bopping. The rock 'n' roll craze had resurfaced, but instead of the old style, we whizzed round in circles while the leader simply hopped from one foot to the other, spinning their partner around.

'C'mon, let's move towards the stage,' he said, 'I want the band to see how beautiful you are.'

Of course, I was soon to realise that it was himself he wanted the band to see! But he was really just another girlfriend to me: he came along when I went pattern and clothes hunting, commenting on styles and fashion, which he was excellent at, and now and again we went to the Sunrise Restaurant on Blackett Street. I always asked for Chicken Maryland, but Ron tried all sorts. He was a waiter at a Newcastle Hotel. One night, he was working a late shift and asked me if I would wait in the kitchen for him to finish. The staff were really friendly; the chef and dishwashers gathered round the table where I was waiting and chatted on. The chef asked if I would like some melba toast. I had never heard of such a thing, but it was lovely, very thin and crusty. Meanwhile, Ron placed a towel across his arm, held a plate aloft on his fingers and swung out between the swing doors.

I was enjoying my snack when the double doors burst open from the dining room and Ron, flushed of face, came raging through. He slammed a steak meal down on the table in front of the chef and announced: 'I have just been humiliated in front of everyone out there by a horrible man, who shouted at me because his steak isn't cooked enough!'

Chef took care of the problem and gave Ron another plate of food. He stood for a second to compose himself, plate in the air and head held high, then lifted the steak and spat underneath before he flourished out to the customer. He loved the work, but hadn't quite cracked the idea that the customer is always right yet.

We hung around together for about ten months, off and on, but one night after we no longer went out, I wasn't at the club and a friend told me that Ron had arrived at the door wearing a dress and make-up. He was turned away. Folks wouldn't have batted an eyelid today, but he was born too soon. He was a lovely lad, I do hope that he eventually found a partner who was just right for him.

* * *

I spent a lot of time at Lena's house. Her mother was German and there were always lovely sausages of all kinds and different types of food, so many flavours. I sometimes stayed over and slept in a bed with Lena and her sister Fran. There wasn't much space so we adopted a position of what they used to call 'Spoons in a drawer'. We all faced the same direction with our knees underneath the one in front's knees. Lena was tidy and kept all of her underwear and clothes ready for that night's outing, while Fran raided the stash of tights and knickers as she never made sure that hers were clean. They were expected to do chores in the home and if they slept too long, their dad shouted up the stairs. It was a regular routine of call and response:

'Yup?' (Are you up?)

'Mup!' (I'm up.)

'Yup yit?' (Are you up yet?)

'Mup noo!' (I'm up now!)

Their mother would then shout, 'Lena unt Fran, downstairs to clean the kitchen!'

We were well into Tamla Motown – 'Baby, Now That I've Found You', 'Bernadette', 'Too Busy Thinking About My Baby' – and Mam was taking herself off to live shows. She went for her usual Friday night hairdo, which was lacquered so much it looked like bell metal. A metal comb with a tail on the end was used to poke it into shape after a night sleeping in her hairnet. *Hair*, the Musical, was showing at the Theatre Royal and Mam went along. At the end, folks were encouraged to dance in the aisles – they threw tiny pieces of confetti into the audience, which became trapped inside her set.

'Mam, aren't you going to comb all of that out?'

'No chance! I only paid for it today, it can stay there until next Friday.'

* * *

One day, I met up with Freda in town and she invited me to her mother's caravan at Amble, a little seaside town. She went there most weekends with a couple of her mates, Lynn and Ann. They all had boyfriends, but definitely only for the season: holiday romances. 'Everlasting Love' was in the charts and I paired up with a lad called Ian, which surprised everyone as he was classed as a loner. A fisherman with a scooter, he was muscly with curly black hair and definitely the quiet, brooding type. Most of the conversation was held by me and after the first date, I thought that was it as there wasn't much feedback. I chattered on regardless and was taken aback when he asked to see me again. Looking back, he was a bit like my dad.

We tagged along with the others to The Schooner and were definitely not popular with the local lasses as they saw us as a threat, taking away the local lads. Freda confided that Lynn's lad only ever surfaced to meet up with her when he could come back to the caravan – we could feel the vibrations coming from the bedroom! He had a car with the registration TUP 634 so he got the nickname 'Tup'. Ian's nickname was 'Meat'! I found that very odd and never called him by this name, but I could see where it originated – he was built like a brick shithouse as the saying goes. Very sweet, though.

'Once you've been out with a lad from here, they expect to meet up with you every time you arrive,' said Freda.

I still wasn't sure that I had made sufficient impression to warrant this, but sure enough, there he was at the harbour.

I bought a suede waistcoat with tassels around the hem, cowboy-style, which fastened with two strips at the front. I wore it with a short-sleeved yellow shirt and suede skirt. Freda borrowed it one night without anything underneath, she was just about inside it. Unfortunately, she had used Immac cream on her underarm hair and hadn't washed it off properly. Massive stains were slimed all over it, so I let her keep it. I didn't suppose anyone would notice what was round her armpits when everything else was on show! We danced to The Byrds and The Yardbirds, but Ian wasn't up for that so I joined the lasses on the floor and he didn't seem to mind. But I was beginning to feel that this relationship wasn't going anywhere when I caught myself wondering what Catherine, Lena, Joan and Jacky were doing – watching a live band at the West End, most likely.

I didn't go back to the caravan, but I did see Ian about six months later when I had begun seeing a new boyfriend. He was standing on the platform of Grey's Monument in town. Usually the space is taken up by religious preachers, Ban the

Bomb, animal rights activists or Women's Lib groups. I've seen rows of knickers strapped around the base of the structure. In the old days, there were brackets which held the trolleybus wires. There he was, looking around: was he meeting some new girl or had he been looking for me? With a new boyfriend, I felt uneasy as I hadn't told him that I wouldn't be back to see him. I'm sure he saw me, but ever the coward, I slinked away into Grainger Arcade to Windows music shop to look for old Jimi Hendrix hits in a purple haze.

John was, as the local saying goes, 'As tight as a fish's arse, and that's watertight'. He never put his hand in his pocket to pay for anything and was continually borrowing money, which was never paid back. The kind who allowed his mates to buy all the rounds and left his own until last, then made an excuse to leave before his turn. I wasn't into sleeping around with lads, I didn't want them to buy me a meal anyway as I thought this meant they might imagine that I would pay for it in some way. I could never understand why lasses said, 'If I don't sleep with him, he said he would chuck me.' As if there was a decision to be made here. Tell him to bugger off then was my way of thinking! I couldn't bring myself to form that kind of a relationship unless I loved the lad, so to this day, I don't know why I did with John. He wasn't very intelligent, or good-looking or even fashionable – we just seemed to drift into dating. Why did I sit there with his mates, knowing that he would sink as many pints as he could and we would be glared at when he said, 'Right then, we're off now!' I didn't accept drinks from them for this reason but it was embarrassing to be going to the bar for my own when he was cadging from all and sundry.

The final straw came when he explained that as he lived with his aunt, she would be very upset if I became pregnant, so if this happened, could I bring the child up at my parents' home and not mention this to her? *Stuff that*, I thought.

I finally woke up and began dating someone else.

CHAPTER NINE

The Divorce

When my brother David was born in 1971, Dad didn't bother to visit him and Mam on the ward and did nothing to prepare for their release from hospital. I painted the kitchen and tried to tidy the miserable flat for Mam, but couldn't help with her feelings of despair. She had been working and had a life apart from Dad, but now she was the trapped one. Being a strong woman, she soon made her own lifestyle and she loved my brother and did her best for him. But she wasn't a natural mother, I knew this, so she took him to relatives in much the same way as I had been brought up. She did attempt to join in with playgroup activities though and volunteered to take the children to the cinema. They were only three years of age and the film was on dinosaurs. They were thoroughly enjoying this and went ranging around the building, impossible to control and round up, so she didn't go back!

It wasn't long after this that she began going out with new men. Her selfish side always grew stronger when she was in a longer-term relationship. A fella called Alan came on the scene; he was older than her and had two twenty-something children. It was near Easter time and Mam took my brother to Woolworths to buy some chocolate eggs. She bought two of the most expensive ones in the store, but they weren't for David. He was only six years of age and he couldn't understand, neither could I or my mam's sister Ellen. But Mam was so taken with this man that her own son came last.

Ellen was furious: 'Doreen, his kids are adults! Why are you buying eggs for them and leaving your own son out?'

Mam took me to meet him: he was a divorcé and lived on his own. He answered the door and went straight into his kitchen, where he was ironing. There were six piles of pressed socks, underpants, shirts, trousers, handkerchiefs and tea towels. They were set exactly the same distance apart in towers on his bench, precisely folded. As she walked across his lino in her stilettos, he cried out that she was making marks on the flooring. She ignored this and proceeded towards the patio doors, which led to the garden. It was raining.

'You must see his garden! He has lovely plants.'

'No, not today, it's muddy outside,' he said.

He was becoming increasingly agitated as she pranced about like a teenager across his highly polished floor, creating little bullet prints as she went. I made my excuses and left, knowing these two were the exact opposites – I couldn't stand the tension. She was the kind who would take her tights off and shove them behind the nearest cushion, drape underwear across the bath and only iron when she needed something to wear. The relationship didn't last long and to my surprise she was devastated. I had never seen her so mismatched with anyone as this Alan, so totally besotted.

* * *

David was also taken to Butlins for his holidays and Mam enjoyed all the preparations – what they would be wearing, etc. One of the new T-shirts she had bought for him was decorated with a *Jungle Book* motif and she warned him not to wear it before the holiday. When Mam came back from work, he was out in the street doing just that. There was such a fight, but Dad couldn't see what all the fuss was about: it was only an item of clothing. He never understood why other people had views different to his own.

At Butlins, Dad was excited to travel on the monorail. It was a piping-hot day and Mam insisted my brother wore a suit – a grotesque blue with scalloped white cuffs – which he hated. She was walking around in a T-shirt and shorts. Dad rolled the jacket up and hid it under the seat with the intention of going back for it later in the day. When they returned, it was gone and hadn't been handed in. Of course, Mam went spare, but the holiday went on as normal – we played the usual games with the Red Coats (my favourite was 'Chuck the Pirate in the Pool') – until Dad caught a stomach bug. They were piled into a taxi and taken home, then he went to hospital. His eyeballs were yellow and he had passed a gallstone.

* * *

My brother told me that one day, when he was at Rutherford School, Stephen – the local bully – was shaking him and his friends down for money. They said they didn't have any, but one lad, Billy, was really scared and showed it. Stephen spat on his hand. There was a covered-in alleyway running from one building to another and it was used on rainy days to prevent pupils from getting wet, so it was nicknamed 'The Cupboard Way' but people avoided it because it was the perfect place to be shoved around. So, one day, Billy didn't want to use the alley and they were walking along Grange Road to get to school when Stephen approached. He was a good-looking lad and loved being fancied by the lasses, all except one who didn't fancy him. This girl was always cuddling my brother – who was only twelve at the time – and she used to ask him if he could get an erection! She was sixteen. For all he tried to avoid her, she was always hanging around him. Stephen was jealous and pinned my brother up against the wall, punching him.

'Stay away from Vicky!'

Once more, David's saviour turned up: Terry worked in the garage across the road from Rutherford School and came to the rescue.

* * *

With so much going on around her, Mam was distraught – she blamed her husband and could take no more. There was a big argument and she threw an ashtray at Dad, which smashed in his face, causing it to bleed. It was one of those sapphire blue glass shells with a silver tray underneath in a shell shape.

Mam had been suffering pain in her side for quite a while before anyone was informed of this – unlike Dad, who reported every last twitch and sneeze. She was admitted to hospital to undergo a gall bladder operation in about 1976 and he never once visited. When she came out, she weighed only seven stone and looked terrible. I was married to my husband David by then and she came to stay with us for a couple of weeks so that I could look after her. When she returned home, Dad wouldn't change his routine at all to help her: he put two teacakes on the table and went out! In time she did regain her strength, but no thanks to him.

They had an argument before the holiday that year and when she refused to go, he went on his own, which suited her fine. She applied for a flat at the Suttons Dwellings, got it and moved half of the furniture and some other things out while he was away. When Mam moved into her new place, she left it to me to explain to my eight-year-old brother that he wouldn't be living at Hampstead Road any more from the following week.

My brother David stayed with us for a while and then while the divorce was going through, he stayed with Dad for three days and with Mam for four days every week. He was only eight years old at the time. This arrangement was not in the least bit comfortable for my brother: PE kits left at one house, forgotten, rushing up and down the village between homes. The divorce was a quickie as neither contested it and she moved out into Suttons Dwellings on the top floor of an estate of flats.

At first, Mam was lonely in the new flat as she had no neighbours around her to be friendly with, so she fell into attending Spiritualist church meetings. I went along to one of those meetings and although it seemed to give folks some kind of comfort, I myself found it very disturbing. The speakers picked someone at random from the congregation to impart some nugget of information. As I've always had a very active imagination, once the light went out at bedtime, I held the covers over my head!

Mam then gave up Spiritualism and became a member of an evangelical church, where she met some good people. They held coffee mornings and craft days. So, was this a radical change? But no, she also ventured into singles clubs, where she met Bob. He approached her and asked if he could buy her a drink, they sat chatting for a while and then when he went to the bar, another woman advised, 'You can't get rid of him if you go out with him once. Steer clear, pet!'

Mam soon found out the meaning of this after initially ignoring the warning. They dated a few times and he offered to decorate her flat and baked her cakes as if to say, 'Now you have no option but to like me'. There was an excuse to call every day. When she became aware of his controlling character, she attempted to finish it. This idea didn't appeal to Bob, so he stalked her and walked backwards and forwards outside her flat. He joined everything she did and even became a member of her church, where he watched every single person who was friendly with her. He persuaded her to stop going, but she simply adopted another church – another evangelical establishment – which annoyed him even more as she began accepting American students into her home to stay while they were studying religious subjects in the UK. He gave the impression that he was OK with it to the young people but once more attempted to put a spanner in the works by asking her out on the nights she went to church. That didn't work so he went along with her.

Each time I visited, he opened his Bible – which was full of bookmarks – which gave the impression that he too was very religious. Both Born-Again Christians, as such they complained about every other sinner. I once pointed out that Mam had had affairs and cheated on Dad.

'Oh, but I don't do that sort of thing now! I've repented and I'm forgiven,' she told me.

Bob persuaded Mam to give up her TV set and preached to my brother, quoting passages from the Bible that spelled out the evils of smoking, drinking and gambling. David disliked him intensely and so moved in permanently with Dad. Mam wasn't settled in the Dwellings so she applied for a bungalow near the city centre, was successful and moved in. This was very attractive to Bob, so he proposed and they were married in 1994. However, the marriage only lasted three years as Mam became ill and was subsequently diagnosed with cancer. Bob was genuinely upset and I felt sorry for him.

* * *

Dad still arranged his possessions in strict order, and even had his meals at exact times. If David went in to start cooking, he moved things around, putting things away before my brother had finished with them. But David thought of a way to avoid this interference: he waited until Dad sat down to eat before he moved into the kitchen. Even then, he would run in to see what was being moved around out of position.

Dad told David how when he was in France with the army during World War II he had come across a deserted mansion, previously inhabited by Germans. There were rifles on the floor. He picked up the rifles and emptied them of all of the ammunition into the chandeliers and walls. No doubt the Germans were blamed for that – it will be written somewhere of the Philistine Germans who destroyed a lovely French home.

David spent most of his time either out with friends, at college, drawing, or in his room, drawing. Dad often had panic attacks, which caused David to cancel lectures. He even managed to throw a wobbler on the day of an important exam. My brother made him promise that it was serious this time – if so, he wouldn't leave until the doctor came. He left the room to get him a drink of water and returned in time to see Dad jump sprightly out of bed to the bathroom to wash his hands. After that, David decided enough was enough.

David's complaints were always met with, 'Well, if you don't like it, you can move out.' And on this day, David did. He informed Dad that he would be moving out at the weekend – he had a flat with his girlfriend, Alison. He didn't go back to see him for about a year, but decided to ask him down to the flat on one occasion for tea. Alison made a chilli meal, Dad said he didn't like it and left the food. Another time, she made chicken in mushroom sauce. He scraped the sauce away and said, 'Next time I come, give me sausage and chips, not this woman's food! And no Chinky-type foreign crap!' David and Alison had given him a chance and once again, he had blown it – they didn't visit him for years after that.

I always bought him Christmas presents, but he never bought us any and said if he didn't like what I had bought – 'I won't wear this', 'Not likely to eat that!'

Had he never heard of saying thanks and taking things back to the shop after Christmas, which is what regular people do, or even donating the gifts to charity?

* * *

Dad regularly went to Butlins on his own, where his favourite haunt was the ballroom. Various dance partners were enlisted, but he didn't socialise with them once the activity ended. He met a woman called Margaret there. She explained that it was her first holiday since her husband had died – he had worked for the Coal Board (in the offices) and had a good pension, so she was comfortable. Then there was Vera – a retired music teacher, she enjoyed musicals and variety shows, so couldn't be better for Dad. She had four grown-up children, three of whom had their own families, and a son in his late thirties still at home.

Dad met up with some people who he saw every year: a father and son, John and Robert from Nottingham, and a woman called Harriet from Holmfirth, his favourite place. He wrote regularly to Harriet, they were all firm friends. He introduced Margaret to them, and after that, they all met every year.

Margaret invited him to stay at her house – she sent him a letter with a hand-drawn map of how to get to her home from the bus station. Dad was on his best behaviour, sat there like Peter Rabbit: he had arrived, he was in *Last of the Summer Wine* country! He came back describing how the food she cooked was superb and how he was saving all his pension for when he got back home. He also noted that her son liked *Star Trek* – now that wouldn't please him at all because he would want to watch his programmes as he did at home: *Dad's Army*, *Last of the Summer Wine*, etc. Only he would know not to rock the boat. We never saw or heard from him around then – he was in his element, staying for six weeks at a time. We also knew that he would never put his hand in his pocket and if he did, the moths would have escaped! I could imagine the scenarios:

'Can I give you something for these theatre tickets? Oh, alright then, if you're sure.' The hand would be rapidly withdrawn from the pocket and nothing more said.

He visited the local swimming baths and went to recitals, where Margaret, being a retired music teacher, played and sang; they also attended operatic society dos and the mixed Probus club for retired or semi-retired folk. They went on holiday regularly, mostly with the people from Doncaster and Huddersfield, who he had met on previous holidays to Butlins. I was really surprised at this because he had never shown any interest in meeting up with other folk, but this was only twice a year and he would have been on his best behaviour. They arranged to meet at Canterbury on one of their holidays, and agreed to take their passports; they travelled to Dover after a few days in Canterbury and took the ferry to France. Other jaunts included a Turkey and Tinsel five-day tour, the Grand Hotel at Scarborough and Blackpool Butlins hotel. Now in his late seventies, he was having a ball.

Dad finally asked Margaret to marry him and she said yes – only, he wanted to move in with her! She explained that it would be better if he got his own flat there until she could sort something out with her son. But he didn't make any move other than to invite Margaret to his flat for a weekend and they decided to go to his local club. She suffered from painful arthritis and he wasn't best pleased when she couldn't get up to dance so he simply asked someone else and left her sitting there among strangers!

That Sunday, they decided to visit the market. Afterwards, he complained to us that, 'It took her ages to walk up the bank!'

He told of a dance session at Margaret's local community centre, where she shared her concerns with him of being a bit overweight. This may have been a ploy to encourage him to enthuse that, no, she was just right. Instead, he pointed to one of her friends who was sitting opposite and said, 'You're not fat! Look at her, *she's* fat.' Whereupon the poor woman left in floods of tears.

He brushed Margaret's concerns aside and the next day, during a walk through the park, went behind a bush to relieve himself. Now, this woman was a retired music teacher, a refined person. When she expressed her concern at this practice, he simply replied that he was ex-army and that was what you did!

By then Dad was suffering from prostate problems and was taking ages to pass water. He consulted the doctor, who advised him to have an operation and so, armed with his overnight bag of pyjamas and toiletries, he arrived at the hospital for his appointment. As he waited for a bed, he began reading the leaflet which explained the details of the operation and the side effects, which included possible difficulties with the sex lives of some patients. He walked out without explaining that he had changed his mind, hence I received another phone call at work from concerned staff. It was left to me to inform them that he had changed his mind.

Margaret contacted him via letter: she explained that although he had asked her to marry him, and she had agreed, as he hadn't made any attempt to move this forward, she was ending the relationship. Anyway, it would affect her pension from her husband and also finish her supply of free coal. So that was that. And please not to call at her house, the suit and shoes he had left behind would be posted on to him.

After Margaret finished the relationship, Dad changed his mind about the prostate operation and assumed if he rang the hospital and told them that he was in agony and unable to pass urine, they would perform the surgery without him having to go on the waiting list again. He was admitted to the Freeman Hospital and I took in a selection of clothing hurriedly chosen from his flat. My brother David agreed to accompany me at visiting time and we walked into the ward, where Dad sat bolt upright in the bed, the picture of health. David noticed that he was wearing a T-shirt which he had screen-printed at college for a project. He turned to me and said, 'I can't believe you brought him a T-shirt that reads "Longshots" in a ward where none of them can have a piss!'

The conversation around the bed revolved around Dad in pathos mood. How he should have married Margaret, and he missed the dancing, swimming, walking, etc., and how he could have been living in a lovely house with a garden with a swimming pool. We reminded him that he had made some pretty offensive remarks about her friends and this was not acceptable and also of the time when Margaret had asked him if she looked overweight at her local church hall. His head leaned to one side, eyebrows raised (not unlike his favourite TV character, Steptoe): 'I know, I shouldn't have said those things, she must have got sick of me.'

Just then a nurse appeared:

'Have you had your urine sample taken yet, Mr Luscombe?'

'Yes, that fat nurse took it.'

Aaargh, give me strength!

Predictably, the test showed that Dad had indeed passed urine that day and he was discharged without further ado, much to his annoyance.

* * *

One evening at home, as I looked through the *Evening Chronicle*, I suddenly spotted him: 'Is that Dad on the front page?'

It surely was. A request had been made from Whitley Bay Lighthouse for volunteers to paint the lighthouse. Dad rode his pushbike from Newcastle's West End, his old work overalls and a paintbrush rolled up on the back of his bike. He was seventy-eight.

On cue he had panic attacks and our continuous round of visits to the hospital resumed, going through the rigmarole of his complaints about the drip attachment they put in his hand in case he needed an operation, after the ECG scans and everything else. I took him back home, bought his shopping – a Kentucky fried chicken meal – and asked him to stay at home for one day to recover. But he never did as he was asked and sprinted out as soon as I left.

I received phone calls at work asking if I could go to Dad's home because he had suffered an attack. My yearly leave allowance was rapidly reduced. The man upstairs to him was annoying him by walking downstairs too loudly. Another time this man had tried to repair a leaking pipe in his bathroom, which had burst and flooded the spare room, previously my brother's room. Again, I took a day's leave to sort it out. Now he was intent on moving house. This became his next topic of conversation, which he talked about obsessively and nothing else. Every time I sympathised, listened and tried to change the subject he simply ignored anything I had to say and went back to his own concerns. I missed calling on him for a few days because of a really bad cold and when I called, he said, 'But I needed some marmalade!'

He was given an application form for warden-controlled

accommodation after a couple of weeks, Anchor housing on Elswick Road. I went to see it – a lovely flat with a communal social room where they served meals during the week, held classes and arranged trips to Harrogate and York. The warden was a decent bloke, what could be better? Dad went for a visit and then began packing, black bags lined his hallway. The next time I went to see him everything was back in its place: he had changed his mind. His mind was made up and changed back twice before he finally moved in. But all was not well: he hated living there.

When a wasp got into one of his slippers and stung his toe, the flat got the blame for that. He washed the windows with neat Domestos and began turning his slippers upside down. He didn't like the lift, he didn't like the bus service, the disabled son of the couple next door or the Scottish man who lived in the building. Another application form for accommodation was sent for.

* * *

Here, David recounts 'The Lock on the Door' story:

'I came back from Europe after a month. When I turned up at the house, the lock which I had always said would break, had: the door was locked solid. [It was a prototype for the plastic deadlock doors that everyone has now.] When I advised Dad to patent it, he said, "What would be the point of that? It wouldn't be a secret then, would it?"

'Anyway, I was locked out, so I proceeded to the local social club where he was holed up to inform him of this, then I went to my mate's house to stay over – I did feel guilty. Instead of

Dad removing the mechanism, he continued to use it, but created another "Secret": he drilled a hole in the window frame and filled it with putty. He would take a screwdriver out with him at all times so that if he was rejected by the door again, he could always use the screwdriver to open the sash window.

'During his time in his flat, predictably, he experienced attacks. The warden sent for the ambulance and again, we carried out the routine of waiting at the hospital for hours as he complained about the bed, nurses, other patients, etc. Our eldest son Gavin went to visit. Dad was asleep on the bed, but he opened his eyes and promptly greeted him with, "Hello Gavin, you're looking fat."

'Dad was discharged, we took him home, collected his shopping, washing and left him in his flat with the customary fast-food meal he preferred. We mistakenly started to take him to the Denton for a couple of drinks once a week to cheer him up, but we soon became suicidal as he ranted and ranted, swearing and cursing about everything on where he was living. At first, we sympathised and tried to change the conversation, but during a three-hour-long evening out, his complaints were the only topic of conversation and this went on for months. David and I came home from work to find a note from Gavin, which read: *The warden of Grandad's flat has left a message, he wants you to write a letter of complaint about the Scottish T**t so that they can evict him.*

'Apparently, this Scottish gentleman had a reputation, complaints were numerous. We wrote the letter, but it didn't make a difference because Dad had already made up his mind to move from there anyway and had begun to visit other properties. He began to reminisce. When he was younger, he would hold onto the bar at the back of the bus and jump off as it was still moving towards the stop [a sort of fairground worker stunt when they jump off and on the dodgem cars]. Unfortunately, he forgot that he wasn't young and fit anymore and duly fell off, hurting his hip and was taken to hospital. After we brought him home, got his shopping and settled him down with a Balti chicken meal, we realised this could be a rest from us going to the pub for an ear-bashing. He was unable to go out for a few weeks, which meant us going to see him more often, but when he recovered, we no longer offered to go to the pub.'

* * *

By now, Bob and Mam had been married for three years and they were quite happy going on rallies with their Christian friends to venues such as the Isle of Mull. Whenever we visited, Bob made sure he had his Bible open – it always displayed dozens of yellow Stickits, giving the impression that he had lots of favourite parts in the Bible and what a devout Christian he was. Mam's sister Ellen would not go to visit her when he was at home and as I've said, even declined the wedding invitation – 'I don't like him, Doreen must be mad to marry him! I'm not going to the wedding because I'd be a hypocrite.'

We often talked about their wedding day at the Civic Centre. Afterwards we all went back to Mam's bungalow

– everyone had chipped in to make the food. There were lots of really nice people there, the sort that were Christian, but didn't pontificate, unlike Bob. He made sure everyone knew that it was wrong to smoke and drink alcohol, but my brother's girlfriend Alison caught him in the kitchen with a fag in his hand, swigging from a bottle of Baileys. She didn't mention this to Mam. Bob later thanked her for not revealing his 'little foibles', but it wasn't for his benefit, she didn't want to upset Mam.

I was standing in the sitting room, talking to some of the guests, when Bob said to me, 'Why don't you sit down?'

When I replied that I was OK as I was talking to my brother, who was also standing, he whispered in my ear, 'Well, the chairs might not be too grand, but they are mine now.'

Mam had experienced pains in her side and we regularly saw her holding the side of her waist, but she never complained, just got on with it. She spent two months in hospital for tests and we visited most nights, going straight from work. Around then we took Dad out for a drink to the pub and as usual, he began complaining about the bus services. When I answered that Mam was very ill and what he was complaining about was a minor thing in life, he replied, 'Well, I don't care! She divorced me, didn't she?'

When we went to pick him up, three days later, he was surprised to see us and observed rather smugly, 'I thought you wouldn't come back after what I said about your ma.'

Bob always came to the hospital and brought his Bible with him. He was ecstatic in reporting a prayer meeting he had attended where the speaker read the Beatitudes. I felt like saying, 'Yeah, those, we did them at school' but restrained myself.

One of Bob's friends accompanied him on this visit and was quite shocked to learn that I often bought a lottery ticket – how sinful to gamble! Again, I wanted to say, 'Yeah, like drinking Baileys and smoking is a sin, Bob.' But I could see how very distressed he was so I held my tongue.

He was really upset to witness Mam's wedding ring fly from her hand across the floor as she raised her hand and took this to be a bad omen. I felt sorry for him, because he was genuinely scared.

When the tests came back, she was told she had liver cancer and it was estimated that she had just two months to live. Because Mam had changed so much since marrying Bob, preferring to be at church most of the time, reading her Bible even when we visited and forgetting to send family birthday cards, she seemed to be distant from us and so I didn't think that I would take this news as badly as I did. The next day, I went to work and tried to get on with things as normal. My boss Debra noticed that I was quiet and when I told her what was wrong, she sent me home immediately.

I was travelling on the bus home when a friend sat beside me. She told me that she had been in Marks & Spencer. She was about to get onto the escalator to go down and a man was in front of her, cleaning his shoes on the brushes at the side of the metal steps. When she got to the bottom, she had noticed that it was my dad. She sniggered at this, but I had other things on my mind – besides, that was normal for him.

Dad must have been thinking about Mam and asked us if he could visit her in hospital. My brother David was concerned that he would say something tactless, but when I told Mam she was pleased that she could make her peace with him (we made sure that Dad would be there when Bob wasn't). Dad was very uncomfortable during the visit, but still mentioned that she shouldn't have had pickle juice! Mam was amused at this, no doubt remembering his antics with the Beechams Powders when he was ill. Of course, drinking pickle juice causes cancer! Mam was discharged home after a month in hospital and a nurse made home visits. Bob was with her all of the time and would interrupt our visits with, 'I think she's getting tired now' – much to the annoyance of Mam, who encouraged us to stay.

Mam's sister Ellen came to visit her in her home and brought her a large bunch of flowers. As I made a move to put them in water, Bob volunteered to do this. Three days later, when I visited, I commented how lovely Ellen's flowers looked. Mam told me that they were a different bunch – there was no water in the vase so the others had died. Bob had spitefully put them in the dry vase to wither.

* * *

For the final two weeks of her life Mam was being cared for at the Marie Curie Centre. It was at this time that Dad secured a warden-controlled flat in the Leazes area. As well as visiting Mam every night straight after work, I was also making new curtains for Dad's flat, cleaning his rooms and helping to move him in.

Bob continued to enjoy holding services in Mam's room at the Marie Curie. Most times we left the room when this was about to take place, but on one occasion Ellen, my son Paul and myself were trapped in the corner on a sofa bed when they came in. One of them began to sing loudly with total disregard for others who were dying in the hospice. There was a pause.

'Amen!'

Ellen belched loudly, then said, 'Oops, it must have been that corned beef and onion sandwich!'

I was sat on the same sofa with Paul and despite the grave circumstances, I could feel the seat bouncing as we stifled our laughter.

* * *

A nurse brought soup and pudding in for Mam on a tray. Bob volunteered to feed her, but she declined, preferring to hold onto her independence. Slowly and shakily, she moved the spoon towards her mouth, then spilt a tiny drop on her nightdress.

'There, you see!' Bob reacted snappily. I sensed he wanted me to intervene, probably so that he could remonstrate with me and ask me to leave, but I just smiled encouragingly to Mam. By now, she was very weak: she held Paul's hand and said how pleased she was to see him. My brother David and sister-in-law Alison, Mam's brothers, John and Leslie, and her sister Ellen were there.

The next time we visited, she was alone, lying on her back

with a Bible placed under her hand – the page was at Psalm 23, 'The Lord is my shepherd'. The nurse told me that Dad had placed it there. I informed her that Bob was not my dad, only married to my mam.

That night I stayed with Mam; she was now being given drugs by syringe driver. Bob was also present and it got to around 9pm. Throughout, he kept wringing his hands and saying, 'Why is it taking so long?'

To which I answered, 'It isn't time yet.'

A nurse came into the room to ask us how we were, to which Bob replied, 'How long is it likely to take?'

She sensitively asked him to step out into the corridor, where she would answer any of his questions, and informed him that hearing is one of the last senses to go and she didn't want Mam to hear their discussion. Marie Curie staff were the best: even when Mam was completely out of it on morphine, they would talk to her gently, telling her what they were going to do.

'We're just changing the bedding now, Doreen, we'll have to move you around a little bit.'

The call that she had died came from Bob at around three o'clock in the morning. I got out of bed so as not to wake everyone, went downstairs and screamed and cried into a pillow. I needed this time alone. Afterwards, when I went back into bed, I don't know if I was dreaming, it felt like a half-asleep and half-awake state, but it felt like she held my hand. Everything around me felt safe and warm.

I went over to break the news to Dad. He bowed his head in customary fashion – he knew there were rules in social situations, ways to behave, and in this case, to offer sympathy. Then he said in a concerned voice, 'Oh, I can see that you are sad. I went to Whitley Bay today and had a chicken dinner for £3.95 with a pot of tea.' His observation of these rules lasted about half a second, then he informed me that he had written a letter to St Dunstans, a housing and nursing care establishment catering for blind ex-servicemen and women.

'But, Dad, you are not blind.'

'I know, but I told them I'm ex-army and served for five-and-a-half years in Germany. I asked if I could come and live there because I'm sick of looking after myself.'

He handed me the brochure, which showed a serviceman sitting in a deckchair. Dad had drawn a hanky on his head with a knot tied in four corners. He had taken to blacking out the teeth of celebrities featured in TV magazines and drawing black glasses on their faces too.

* * *

Bob confided that he couldn't face clearing the bungalow of Mam's personal effects so I volunteered to do this and he suggested it was done when he was out. She had very little in the way of clothing, mostly old, worn things, and she had sent most of her money to these 'students' of religion who had often came to stay with her – she fed them and always sent donations, mostly to America. There was a new navy jacket which I tried on, but after the first time of wearing it, I felt like I was wearing her, if that makes sense. She seemed to be ever-present, so I gave it away.

Among her possessions I found two records: 'Tie A Yellow Ribbon Round The Old Oak Tree' and 'Please Release Me' by Engelbert Humperdinck. There was an old purse with some money inside, so I left it where it was. Also, a silver locket, which I had bought her with my first week's wages, so I took that and a broken set of glass beads. The photos of our family would mean nothing to Bob, so I took those too. We gave a Sowerby ornamental glass bowl to my uncle John, Ellen was given some dressing-table glassware (these items were made by her brother Willy when he was a glassblower at the factory), her wedding hat went to my brother David and anything we thought Bob wouldn't want went to charity shops. He was grateful for our help, but commented that the one thing which upset him most was when he discovered the purse. Bugger, I hadn't meant to upset him!

Mam's friends were very caring people, they always had a kind word to say. They spoke about the trips out they shared together and how even when she was in pain, she still called in to the church to help with changing the flowers and cleaning the hall.

The funeral was arranged by David and me. We cashed her policies to pay and Bob used a policy they had paid for together for the wake, which was to be held at the church hall they had frequented. On the day of the funeral the family arranged to meet at Mam's house. It was here that I discovered that the pastor who was to take the service was an ex-police inspector. This became evident from the style of his preaching – all hell, fire and brimstone. As our family were in the front row, and none of us were churchgoers, we distinctly felt that his comments were directed at us – how we needed to repent, go to church and suchlike. I couldn't help but think of what he himself might need to repent: why had he become a church leader? Could it be that in his past he had a few things on his conscience? Meanwhile, in reply to everything he uttered, the congregation all chanted phrases in unison, such as 'Yeah, lord', 'Praise be' and 'Mercy be'.

Bob gave me the engagement ring he had bought her. I gave it to my sister-in-law, Alison – the locket and the broken beads were enough for me. I gave Mam's first wedding ring when she was married to our dad to my brother David.

At the graveside, Bob decided to hold an impromptu service, oblivious to the fact that the gravediggers were leaning on their shovels and the funeral directors were due at another family home. He also gave a long speech about how he was chosen to be with Mam and his religion would save him, and that we should all be happy that she was going to a far better place. This went on for some considerable time. Luckily for Bob, the funeral director decided not to charge him extra.

Meanwhile, back at the church hall, two of Mam's friends spoke after the pastor's speech. It was an immense comfort to me to hear of her favourite places, the things she liked to do and their memories of good times together. Afterwards, the pastor approached me and was angling for a glowing report on his sermon. I said that I had enjoyed hearing Mam's friends offering words of comfort and was about to move off when out of the corner of my eye, I spied Dad. *Oh, no!* He listened to everything that was said and then piped up, 'They said some nice things about Doreen, but did you know that she threw an ashtray at me, which cut my head?'

I shot Dad a look and told him that this was not the place to talk of such things. But that didn't deter him and he added, 'Well, I was married to her for twenty-nine years and he was only married to her for three-and-a-half!'

Mam's friends had worked very hard in preparing the food: it was a cold November day and they served everyone with hot chicken and baked potatoes, lots of rice and other tasty things. I made the mistake of not sitting within elbow distance of Dad. During the partaking of the meal, I overheard him slagging off Willy, Mam's brother, who had died two years before from cancer. Dad was informing one of the guests that Willy had never done a decent day's work in his life and that he used to call him 'idle swine', to which he began singing 'idle swine' to the tune of 'Edelweiss' from *The Sound of Music*. Fortunately, the person's mobile went off, bringing an end to that conversation.

Our family left the hall and went to my brother's flat to wind down. It had been a day and a half. Gavin went home. After a couple of hours, we received a phone call from him: he had tried to open a stiff garage door and badly cut his face. So, it was off to the A&E department at Newcastle General Hospital. Gavin was in one cubicle, having stitches in his face, and his girlfriend was in the one next door, having fainted at the sight. Roll on tomorrow!

At least something was in our favour: Dad was in his

element at his new flat. The bus route was still pleasing him, the neighbours so far were OK – although he didn't speak to any of them, which is how he liked it. After a while he did pass the time of day with an elderly Chinese man called Mr Wu, an extremely well-mannered, friendly person. He placed a wonderful orange lily plant in the hallway of the block of flats. Dad was also presented with a portable television set – Mr Wu explained that he had won it at his club (he already had one so he didn't need it), to which Dad replied, 'It hasn't been pinched, has it?'

Poor Mr Wu was mortified.

A week on, Dad decided that he didn't need the TV either. He offered to sell it to me for £20. One week later, he rang to say he shouldn't have sold it. Here was I assuming he was going to give me the money back, but no, he thought that he could have got more for it, had he sold it privately.

Dad went to Whitley Bay again and this time he used his compass while travelling – 'It changes to North when I turn the corner.' He shopped at Marks & Spencer and saved all of the sticky labels, which he stuck to the tiles in his kitchen, 'In case I run out of Sellotape.' He went to the Metrocentre, the huge shopping centre in Gateshead, and sometimes wasn't back when we called. Because everything in his world appeared to be rosy, it was a great surprise to receive a call from the warden, Muriel at Dad's home, informing us that he had suffered an attack. Apparently, the neighbour downstairs had made a complaint regarding Dad's habit of singing loudly at 6.30am. Banging his toothbrush against the sink and just about taking the bottom out of his cup whenever he stirred his tea were among other strange habits. This neighbour also complained about his feeding of the birds. Muriel explained that this woman was highly-strung – unfortunate for her to live downstairs from my dad. The conversation I had with the warden was embarrassing because I felt that she would think I was heartless as I explained to her about the 'Cry wolf' scenarios. However, she soon experienced this for herself when Dad pulled the emergency cord to ask for his shoelaces to be tied.

Muriel told me of the mad panic when he pulled the cord, shouting for the doctor. She contacted the doctor, but when he arrived, Dad kept him waiting for fifteen minutes. The doctor alerted Muriel because he could not gain access to the flat. A spare key was obtained from the office and when they rushed in, they discovered Dad quite happily drinking a cup of tea.

'Mr Luscombe, why didn't you answer the door?' said Muriel.

'Because I was eating my cornflakes,' he announced calmly.

His card was now well and truly marked.

* * *

After each subsequent customary hospital visiting routine we again settled him down, told him to stay put for a couple of days to recover, but no, he was off to Whitley Bay on the Metro the very next day. As we had always predicted, he cried wolf once too often. I was called from work to his flat, but on expecting much of the same, I was confronted by Dad being helped into a wheelchair. His vision on one side was impaired, he couldn't walk and looked completely out of it. At the hospital a young doctor carefully removed his jumper to reveal one of his T-shirts bought from a charity shop. It displayed two Bulldogs shagging and read 'Hot Dog Relish'.

We were told that Dad had suffered a mini stroke. The medication he was on caused hallucinations, which to him ranged from coffins, bodies being dragged along the floor by nurses, the blood pressure machine spying on him and twelve glasses of water coming towards him. When a nurse came to give him his tablets, he said, 'Oh, there are twelve of you, they're all big! *You're* big, aren't you?'

When the nurse left, he told us that a party of student doctors had surrounded his bed to ask questions.

'They asked me who was the Prime Minister and I told them, Tony Clair.'

We soon discovered that he lost his temper when we couldn't get the drift of his conversation.

'They gave me one of those yellow things.'

Blank looks.

'You know, man. Not round, oval, you put them in your tea.'

'Lemon.'

'That's right, melon! No, it was a banana.'

He continued to speak loudly about cringingly embarrassing subjects and to discuss everyone's business in a very inappropriate manner.

'That man over there's an alcoholic and he's a diabetic; I

don't know what the darkie's in for. That bloke over there pees on the floor in the toilet. You can't see the darkie when all of his visitors come because there are so many of them around the bed.'

What he didn't realise was that all of that family were there because that man was loved. His family fed him, offered him drinks, adjusted his pillow, combed his hair and only left when the nurses gave the signal.

Nobody else wanted to be there with Dad – my brother had given up and my two sons came just occasionally (Paul would have visited more often, but he was living in Cambridge). One small consolation was to observe the patient in the next bed to Dad. When his son came in, he said loudly, 'It's murder in here, all the noisy sods!'

His son cringed and nipped the bridge of his nose in pure embarrassment. So, I wasn't the only one! The nurse informed me that Dad's blood pressure was high and that he would not be discharged until it was back to normal. She added that he had been getting out of bed, going for brisk walks up and down the corridor and doing star jumps in the lounge against the advice of the staff. My husband David and I tried to convince him that he would not be going home unless he did as he was told. However, on our next visit, we were informed by the staff nurse that he had fallen and cut his head, which required stitches after one of his jumps went wrong. All we heard from him was that he was trying to keep fit. No amount of persuasion to relax was taken in and so he remained in hospital for longer than he would have liked.

* * *

I arrived at visiting time one day to find Dad highly agitated by a poor patient on his ward who was finding it extremely difficult to breathe and was obviously also in a great deal of pain.

'I'm f*****g sick of him making all this noise!'

'Dad, do not swear in here, where people are genuinely ill! If you did as you were asked by the nurses, you could go home – this poor man hasn't a choice.'

'He kept me awake all f***ing night!'

'Dad, if you continue to be abusive, I'm going to walk out.'

'Well, I'm f***ing sick of him!'

I stood up and made my way towards the door. My husband David was unsure what to do – he looked from me to Dad, and eventually got up to go too, having explained to him why I had left. When I glanced back on my way out there was not one flicker of concern on his face. I informed the nurse that I would not be visiting again until Dad was discharged and asked her if she would tell him. I was beginning to feel very stressed by all of this – being called from work, having to visit and keeping his home as well as my own. None of this I would have objected to, had he taken good medical advice and been more sympathetic of others.

* * *

Once more we picked him up from hospital, stocked his fridge and made sure that the tablets were sorted into the week planner. He turned to me and said, 'You LEFT me in the hospital!'

I flew into a temper and asked him why he thought that that was, but he had no recollection of his behaviour, so I launched into an attack, hopelessly attempting to make him understand.

'OK, imagine you're sitting on the bus with a nice little old lady from next door and I get on the bus and come out with, "I'm f***ing sick of my boss, she's a f***ing s***faced b*****d!" How would you feel then, hmmn?'

No reaction from him, but David's mouth fell open and he was speechless. If we were ever thinking of inviting Dad to live with us, all thoughts were dispelled after my husband invited him to go on holiday with us that year. We booked a cottage on the Downalong in St Ives, Cornwall. There were three bedrooms so we also asked my brother David and his wife Alison.

Dad bought himself a new watch with an expandable strap. He didn't like the design, so he stretched it across the door handle to make it slacker.

'Dad, you could leave that watch there until hell freezes over and it still won't alter the size! That's what expandable watches do. It will go straight back to its original size when you remove it from the door handle, man,' I told him.

But he ignored this and left it where it was.

He also collected clocks and had fifteen altogether. One of them, his latest, was a digital speaking affair in the design of a crash helmet.

'What's it saying "Peema Pema" all the time?'

I set it to alarm and it spoke in an American accent.

'Dad, it's saying 6pm.'

He told me that when he was a kid, they were too poor to afford a clock and each day, he was sent to the downstairs neighbour to ask the time – he hated doing it.

'Bugger to hell! When are you lots going to get your own clock?'

It was a ten-hour journey and I was beginning to be aware that all was not going to be well when Dad commented on the appearance of his fellow passengers.

'Look at the kite [stomach] on him!' – regarding a stout gentleman who passed his seat. He showed annoyance when anyone came to sit in the seat near him. Alison spent the rest of the journey with her coat over her head.

David paid for the taxi to the cottage, we dumped our cases, then called to a local Spar to fill up the fridge. Inside the shop we split up to forage and returned to the checkout with our food. David and Alison took chicken, peppers, cream, peppercorns, rice, pasta, bottles of wine, toiletries, etc. David and I bought bacon, eggs, sausages, cakes, cheese, biscuits, milk, sugar, etc. Dad turned up with a packet each of Jaffa Cakes and Hobnobs.

Back at the cottage, we chose our rooms. David and Alison had the queen-sized room, we moved into the king-sized and Dad settled into the twin bedroom at the back of the building. That evening, we took him out for a meal. Alison ordered lobster, David and I had steak and my brother David chose fish. Dad ordered a starter and proceeded to eat our vegetables!

The next day, David and Alison confided that they had had a restless night – the bed was too small for the two of them. They asked Dad if he would swap his twin room. Grudgingly, he agreed. They were pleased with the move, but Dad complained the next day that he had got used to his own room and didn't like their room. Alison agreed to move back that evening, but when they were out, Dad shifted all of their possessions out and his own back in. They were annoyed: why couldn't he have waited until their return?

That evening, we decided to go to a lovely restaurant called the Blue Fish. The food was delicious, but again, Dad ordered a starter and helped himself to our food. Two Frenchwomen were enjoying a meal nearby and Dad announced, 'What a stink of garlic!' He embarrassed my brother by returning what was left in his glass to the empty bottle of 7 Up, then placed the bottle in his pocket.

'I'll have that later.'

When in an old Cornish village, most folk accept that there are narrow streets with no pavements in certain areas. But Dad didn't, he insisted on walking in the middle of the tiny narrow lanes, and when a car came behind him, he became highly agitated. He complained about the sea frets, the heavy-duty frying pan and about Alison's cooking, but didn't offer to contribute in any way. He got out of bed at 6.30am and banged his toothbrush dozens of times on the side of the sink (what was in there, the Adriatic?). He arranged the cutlery, crockery, the kettle, etc. all in regimental order, stirred his tea loudly, clanking the spoon at least ten times one way, ten times the other, and then in a circular motion rapidly for at least thirty revolutions.

The World Cup was being shown on TV that week so Dad slipped into loner mode and didn't bother going out with us on an evening for the rest of the week. He was perfectly happy, feet up on the coffee table, wearing his Santa socks in the middle of June. My brother deduced that he had been awkward on purpose to resume his habitual lifestyle. Crafty, eh? That night, the four of us went for a spicy Mexican meal – it was great! We went on to a live band gig, where we met another couple from Manchester – Dad wouldn't like having to be in the company of 'strangers'. After a brilliant night out, we said goodbye to the couple and went for a stroll around the beautiful streets. There was not another soul around so we went down onto the beach of a little cove, where all we could hear was the lapping of the waves as we stood without shoes in the cool water, watching the light from Godrevy Lighthouse going around in the bay. Peace, perfect peace!

When we got back to the cottage, Dad was in bed so my brother David, being slightly merry, suggested we clank a spoon around in a cup for a while. We laughed at the orderliness of everything on the work surfaces and my husband noted the position of the kettle, next to the cup Dad had chosen: 'Take the cup to the kettle, not the kettle to the cup.'

Dad was always saying this so my brother promptly unplugged the kettle and put it in a different position. That was his way of gaining revenge for the bathroom routines and singing torture he had suffered on this holiday.

'I come on holiday to relax and have a lie-in, not to be

woken up at this unearthly hour, I'll be doing twenty-five years after this,' he said.

The next day, David and Alison decided on a peaceful day at the harbour in St Ives – they hired a speedboat – so my husband and I asked Dad if he wanted to come with us on a trip to Boscastle and Jamaica Inn. He declined and so we had a stress-free day and met some lovely people who were on a Saga holiday. Claire was a widow and holidayed on her own; she was staying at the Porthminster Hotel and lived in Hull. Then there was a woman called Elizabeth, who was in her seventies, accompanied by a man called Colin, who we assumed to be her son, but he was about thirtyish and he was her husband. We were so pleased that Dad was not there to hear this! We had also booked another trip to Falmouth and Truro, to which Dad had agreed to accompany us. I secretly hoped that Elizabeth and Colin would not be there, for their sakes. Claire, however, was there and as we were talking to her before boarding the coach, Dad was hovering behind us. She lowered her head and quietly remarked, 'I don't wish to alarm you, but there is a rather strange man listening to us.' I looked around to witness Dad standing sideways, his head inclined towards us. It would never have occurred to him to join in or present himself to her, ready to be introduced. 'Yes, that's my dad,' I replied. She immediately offered a profusion of apologies. I told her not to worry about it. Dad made it quite clear that he didn't appreciate her 'intrusion' by acting like a child, showing impatience and staring at her, narrowing his eyebrows and hopping from one foot to another, and so we continued with the trip as a trio.

Dad had more or less decided to continue with his solitary walks around the coast, so we didn't hear much more of the complaints until the last day of the holiday when we discovered he had made a complaint to the owners of the cottage about the frying pan. The train journey back was also no picnic as he complained as usual – the two young mothers with a young baby each didn't best please him. The babies travelled with us for the next eight hours as the mothers sang repeated refrains of 'The Wheels On The Bus'. We sat through more comments about the other passengers and narrowly missed being attacked, but otherwise remained unscathed. After we had dropped Dad off at home and collected his shopping and settled him in, we heaved a sigh of relief on the way home. We decided that we would never again take him on holiday, but day trips would be acceptable.

* * *

That year, we invited Dad as usual for Christmas lunch and picked him up at five past twelve, our agreed time having been twelve o'clock. After being admonished for being late, David muttered under his breath, 'It's not beam me up, Scottie!'

We busied ourselves serving lunch while Dad drank a Baileys, watched *Rising Damp* and *Duty Free*. Throughout the day, his list of programmes included *In Loving Memory*, *Only When I Laugh* and *Last of the Summer Wine*. Although he had the money, he would not have a telephone or invest in Sky TV, even though he could watch all of his favourites on UK Gold.

After Dad ate lunch, which consisted of turkey, roast and

boiled potatoes, five veg, cranberry sauce and mint, followed by Christmas pudding in white sauce and two glasses of Asti, then endless supplies of nuts, chocolate caterpillar cake, etc., he remarked, 'Well, I could have had that dinner at Fitzgerald's for £3.95.' What a cheek! Then he asked if he could take some turkey home in a Tupperware for the next day. As David took him back home at around 7pm, Dad took great delight in complaining to him about the paper cuts on his hands inflicted as he had put his Christmas cards in his pocket.

We spent an enjoyable complaints-free Boxing Day and the next day, I arranged to spend a day in town with my friend Irene. We bought craft equipment, looked at fabrics, had lunch with Irene's cousin in the Laing Art Gallery restaurant – a great day out. When I set foot inside the door back home, there had been a phone call from Muriel: Dad had complained to her about a sore arm and he was back in hospital. I rang the hospital and spoke to the ward nurse. She said that he was fine, enjoying his food, so to ring back in an hour.

When we arrived at the hospital the nurse confided that Dad hadn't been taking his tablets, hiding them instead, so they had to stand over him until he took them. David was angry and said to him in no uncertain terms, 'Ken, that's why you're back in here again! You're not taking your tablets and you'll keep coming back until you're dead, that's what will happen, you'll die!'

'Have you got any of that turkey left?' he said. 'I thought you might have brought some in?'

We stayed for just over an hour, then I explained to him

that I was going to have a word with the nurse before I left. As I was speaking to her in the corridor, Dad sidled up to us and was earwigging, so she addressed him directly: 'I was just telling your daughter about how you haven't got much movement in your arms.'

Gesturing towards David, Dad said, 'He said that I'm in here because I didn't take my tablets, is that right?'

'Oh, yes, Ken, you must take them every day,' she told him.

After he was discharged, the fridge had been stocked by us once more, etc., etc., and we made a point of making sure that his medipack was fully stocked with tablets. We went for our own shopping and returned to Dad's flat only to find that he had flushed the tablets down the toilet. We had spares and I watched as he put them in his mouth. He took a drink to help them down, then disappeared to the bathroom. We looked at each other knowingly: the old stoat had spat them out! Sure enough, this carried on until he again suffered another mini stroke. In the past, conversations with Dad had always been a mixture of fact, the present and the past, but since this latest episode, they became more rambling. And as usual, the things he told us were not meant for feedback, only as statements.

We called on him one day after work and he was sawing through a long spoon, which was meant for use in tall ice-cream sundae glasses.

'Dad, why are you sawing that?'

'It's too big.'

'But you have about forty teaspoons, why do you need another?'

'I bought this one in a charity shop because I like it.'

I couldn't believe it when David became involved in this.

'Here, Ken, hand it over, I'll do it.'

But Dad still couldn't relinquish the task fully and kept holding onto the saw. David continually asked him to let go. He sat there for around half an hour, sawing and sweating like a pig. At last it was through.

'Ken, have you got a file?'

Dad foraged in his toolbox and returned, file in hand. Another ten minutes was spent smoothing the edges and when it was finished, he retreated to the kitchen and we heard the kettle boiling. He came back in with a cuppa and the spoon was peeping over the top by a couple of centimetres.

'It's too big!'

* * *

Dad sent for free gifts from adverts in newspapers and magazines but had no intention of taking up the membership conditions. There were free pens for switching computer service providers when he didn't own a computer and a free clock for becoming a member of a book club. He received the first book, paid for it and refused to accept any others as part of the agreement.

Dear Mr Luscombe,
You have accepted our free gift and ordered one book and haven't ordered any subsequent books from our collection. If there are none from our titles which

interest you, could you please advise us of any authors in which you may be interested.

They were treated to a reply which told them to '*F*ck off!*' The amount of times I gave up my break time at work to call companies to explain and get him out of it…

We were treated to a selection of his mixed-up conversations, usually spoken when he had one eye on the television, sitting there wearing a 'Free Nicaragua' T-shirt, pontificating on all and sundry.

'The woman from the Post Office left a card… Have you seen those featherless chickens, it says [the TV] that it will save the starving people. I think it's just a gimmick for these fast food sellers. It's a good pen – someone left it and I just picked it up in the bookies at Whitley Bay. I had a couple of bets on: 6–1 on Flying Romance. The other two went down, I put £1.00 treble on. I think the foot and mouth disease has been brought over here by the asylum seekers…'

* * *

As Dad's dementia became more advanced, I applied for respite at the Connie Lewcock Resource Centre. The social worker arranged this and explained that they would assess him: he would be observed on how well he could make himself a cup of tea, understand his surroundings and a report would be made. He would only be there for one day, but when I visited, he called me all the names under the sun.

'You've put me in here, you t**t!'

'This isn't permanent, Dad. The staff are only assessing you. And it's to give me a break.'

'So, you mean I can leave any time I like?' he said, eyes darting back and forth. 'Right then, I'm out of here!'

He packed his bag and we took him back to his flat.

There were numerous scares: he set fire to the cooker, the fire brigade were called, he continued to annoy the neighbours and fell off his bike as he weaved in and out of traffic. I honestly imagined this was how he would end his days, murdered by a neighbour or in a motorway pile-up.

* * *

A doctor at the hospital became interested in Dad: he was carrying out research and making a report on the elderly and Asperger syndrome. I attended a meeting after he had interviewed Dad and my part was to relate family stories and fill in a questionnaire. After the report was completed, I received a document with a breakdown of Dad's condition, along with another half-dozen men who displayed traits and obsessions too. One man collected dozens of ties and never wore any of them, another wore nappies as he was afraid of breaking wind.

Dad was finally diagnosed.

Eventually he was assessed after many more falls and mini strokes. We chose a care home where he continued to wreak havoc. Staff simply put it down to dementia, little knowing he had always been like this. He collected carrier bags if he could get his hands on them and stuffed them under chair cushions; he was wearing a urinary catheter and if the staff didn't change it to his liking, he simply stripped off and stood in the nip in the corridor until someone attended to him. He befriended a giant of a man called Ken, who had lost the power of speech and couldn't feed himself. Dad watched him chase a pea around his plate then stepped in to feed him. The poor man couldn't hold a regular cup and drank tea from a two-handled Tommee Tippee mug with a lid on and Dad held it for him.

When I visited, he could be found picking the paint from the hand rails in the corridor. The man next door called Bill imagined that he was in a social club when he was in the dining room – he always asked me if I wanted a drink, rummaged through his pockets and brought out the white lining.

'Oh, I'm sorry, pet, I've got no money – the bloke next door owes me £20 and I haven't had my wages yet.'

'It's OK, Bill, here are a few coppers to keep you going,' I said and he went off happy.

There are some sad sights in these places: women holding dolls wrapped in crochet blankets, asking when the nappies are due to arrive, and people hanging around the door, waiting for a parent to take them home. One day, when Bill approached, he handed me a tube of sweets.

'Do you want one?'

'Yes, please, Bill.'

Bill put the tube in his pocket and we continued chatting about how he had just finished his shift down the pit. He foraged through his pocket to find the sweets once more and brought out a pair of underpants. He was a canny soul, but he too began deteriorating. Usually always smart, his jacket was now covered in food stains and he regularly wore it with the hanger still inside and the hook at the back of his head.

* * *

One Friday, I was at work when the call came that Dad had slipped into a coma and I rushed straight there to be at his bedside. I stayed there all night, holding his hand with no response. Then, at around eleven o'clock, he sat bolt upright in bed, gazing at the ceiling with a look of absolute wonder, mouthing what looked like 'Mam!' I was in terror at this, only the light from a small lamp on. I'd never witnessed anyone dying before and wondered what it was that he could see in the room. I lowered my head while still holding his hand and he flopped down. *Was this his time?* I couldn't tell, but all of a sudden when I felt the most fear, a warmth covered my whole back and I felt peaceful. There is no explanation for this: was it my system taking over to calm me, was there someone there with us? I will never know.

What had Dad witnessed? Was it really his mother, or was it because his pupils had dilated and allowed light in so that everything appeared bathed in light? Surely, from what I knew, this happens at the moment of death, but he was still with us until the Sunday. He and my brother had fallen out and I rang to ask if David would come to the home. This he did and we both recounted stories to Dad from our memories. He opened his eyes and gazed from one to the other, his eyes were smiling and then he slipped into peace. We drew the curtains and left the room. Bill next door was in the hallway, shouting,

'Someone's pinched my sweets!' and a woman was distressed as her daughter had gone down in the lift without her.

I was not going to miss this place.

* * *

Dad's possessions were taken out on a trolley – we didn't want anything except the tapes which he had recorded when my brother was about eight. We took them away and that night, me and my brother put them onto an old recorder.

'If I came into the room when he was recording,' said David, 'he switched it off.'

We listened for most of the night. Dad was telling stories in German, French and Italian, telling jokes, singing his favourite songs. One tape was made around the time Mam had left him and the music was Cliff Richard's 'We Don't Talk Anymore', *Pagliacci* and 'We'll Gather Lilacs'.

Typically, there is a story about a fat woman who couldn't get through the door to board a train and a guard pushed her from behind. Another of a very rich man on a huge yacht, who looks down on a tiny boat where the owner is cooking a juicy steak and the aroma wafts up.

'Tell me, my man, how can you make such a lovely steak?'

'When you own a small boat like this, you can afford to buy the best steak!'

I've often pondered why I didn't understand him despite the fact that he had Asperger syndrome: would it have made any difference if I had known this earlier? These two stories summed him up exactly – a loner, his obsession with overweight people and how he was happy to live with very little. Why had it taken longer to get over his death than that of Mam? 'Because she didn't make you feel guilty,' said David. I still don't know, but he was special in his own way and he taught us both to draw and paint. Now, my brother sells his amazing oil paintings and I tell stories.

Thanks, Dad.

Acknowledgements

Thank you firstly to my brother, David, and all my family and friends featured in this book, as well as Dave Morton of the *Newcastle Chronicle*, Mike Young at the West Newcastle Picture History Collection for your support and research on photos from the collection, Keith Fisher and Shawn Fairless for your help with the photographs, and the Discovery Museum, Tyne Bridge Publishing and Summerhill Books. Thank you also to Sarah Fortune at John Blake Publishing and Jane Donovan for your support and guidance.

Introducing a new place for story lovers – somewhere to share memories, photographs, recipes and reminiscences, and discover the very best of saga writing from authors you know and love, and new ones we simply can't wait for you to meet.

A new address for story lovers

www.MemoryLane.club